THIS IS
NEW ZEALAND

THIS IS
NEW ZEALAND

Text by David Wall

Photographs by David Wall and Holger Leue

NH
NEW
HOLLAND

First published in 1999 by
New Holland Publishers (NZ) Ltd
Auckland • Sydney • Cape Town • London

218 Lake Road
Northcote, Auckland, New Zealand

14 Aquatic Drive
Frenchs Forest, NSW 2086, Australia

80 McKenzie Street
Cape Town 8001, South Africa

24 Nutford Place
London W1H 6DQ, United Kingdom

ISBN 1 85974 089 8 (hard cover)

ISBN 1 86436 522 6 (soft cover)

Commissioning Editor & Editor: Simon Pooley
Publishing Manager: Mariëlle Renssen
Designer: Dean Pollard
Cartographer: John Loubser

Reproduction by Unifoto (Pty) Ltd
Printed and bound in Singapore by Tien Wah
Press (Pte) Ltd

10 9 8 7 6 5 4 3 2 1

Illustrations appearing in the preliminary pages
are as follows:

HALF TITLE: Adrian Peeni, Maori carver,
at Thames, Coromandel Peninsula.
FRONTISPIECE: A view of Mt Taranaki from Lake
Mangamahoe, near New Plymouth, Taranaki.
TITLE PAGE: Maori cultural festival, Ruatahuna.
THIS PAGE: Maori whalebone carving, Rotorua.
PAGE 5: View from the Sky Tower, Auckland.

ACKNOWLEDGEMENTS

The Author would like to express his gratitude to
the following for their generous and valuable
assistance: Jude, my wife, has given me enormous support throughout all stages of the
photography, writing and editing of this book.
Both of our families have also helped in many
ways. A number of people and companies have
assisted me greatly in obtaining photographs.
Some of these include Nick Andreef of Waitomo
Adventures; Waitomo Glow Worm Caves; Whaka-
rewarewa Village, Rotorua; Waiotapu Geothermal
Wonderland; Gannet Safaris, Hawke's Bay; Te Papa
Museum, Wellington; Jeff Thomson, artist; Montana
Wines, Blenheim; Whale Watch, Kaikoura; the
Wizard of New Zealand, Christchurch; Mountain
Jade, Hokitika; Alex Millar, pilot, Mount Cook Line;
Franz Josef Glacier; Alpine Guides Fox Glacier;
Otago Rugby Union; Penguin Place, Otago Penin-
sula; Otago Museum, Dunedin; Hocken Library,
Dunedin; Coronet Peak Skifield; and Kiwi
Wilderness Walks.

The Editor would like to thank Belinda Cooke
and Renée Lang of NHP (NZ) for their assistance.

PHOTOGRAPHIC ACKNOWLEDGEMENTS

Auckland City Libraries (NZ): pp31, 32 (top
right & bottom left)
**Hocken Library, University of Otago,
Dunedin:** 33 (top)
Holger Leue: pp 2; 3; 4; 13; 25 (top); 37; 43 (top);
50 (top); 51 (top right); 53 (top right & bottom); 54
(bottom); 56 (top); 57 (top & bottom right); 58 (top &
bottom); 59 (middle & bottom); 60 (top & bottom);
61 (bottom); 63; 65 (top & bottom); 67 (bottom); 69
(bottom); 72 (bottom); 73 (top & bottom); 75; 78;
79 (bottom); 80 (top); 81; 89 (top left & right); 90
(top right); 92 (bottom left); 94; 96 (top & bottom);
97; 99 (top & bottom); 104 (top left); 112 (bottom);
114 (bottom); 116 (bottom); 117 (top); 122
(bottom); 124 (top); 126 (top); 127 (bottom); 133
(bottom); 135 (top); 137 (top & bottom); 139 (bottom); 141 (bottom right); 159 (top); 163 (top &
bottom); 170 (top left & bottom); 171; 172 (top)
Jean du Plessis: 134 (left)
Photobank Image Library: 29 (top)

DEDICATION
To all those who by visiting New Zealand's
spectacular wilderness, ensure its preservation.

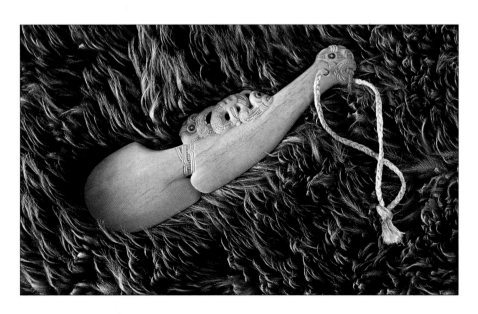

CONTENTS

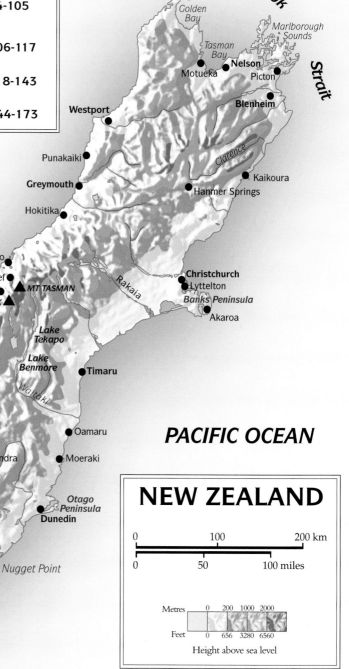

TASMAN SEA

Cook

Cape Farewell

Golden Bay

Marlborough Sounds

Tasman Bay

Motueka

Nelson

Picton

Strait

Westport

Blenheim

Punakaiki

Clarence

Kaikoura

Greymouth

Hanmer Springs

Hokitika

South Island

Okarito

Christchurch

Franz Josef

Lyttelton

Fox Glacier

▲ MT TASMAN

Rakaia

Banks Peninsula

MT COOK ▲

Akaroa

Jackson Bay

Lake Tekapo

Lake Benmore

Timaru

Lake Wanaka

Milford Sound

Waitaki

Lake Dunstan

Oamaru

PACIFIC OCEAN

Queenstown

Lake Te Anau

Lake Wakatipu

Alexandra

Moeraki

Clutha

Otago Peninsula

Dunedin

Catlins

Nugget Point

Invercargill

Foveaux Strait

Bluff Harbour

Halfmoon Bay

Stewart Island

NEW ZEALAND

0	100	200 km

0	50	100 miles

Metres	0	200	1000	2000
Feet	0	656	3280	6560

Height above sea level

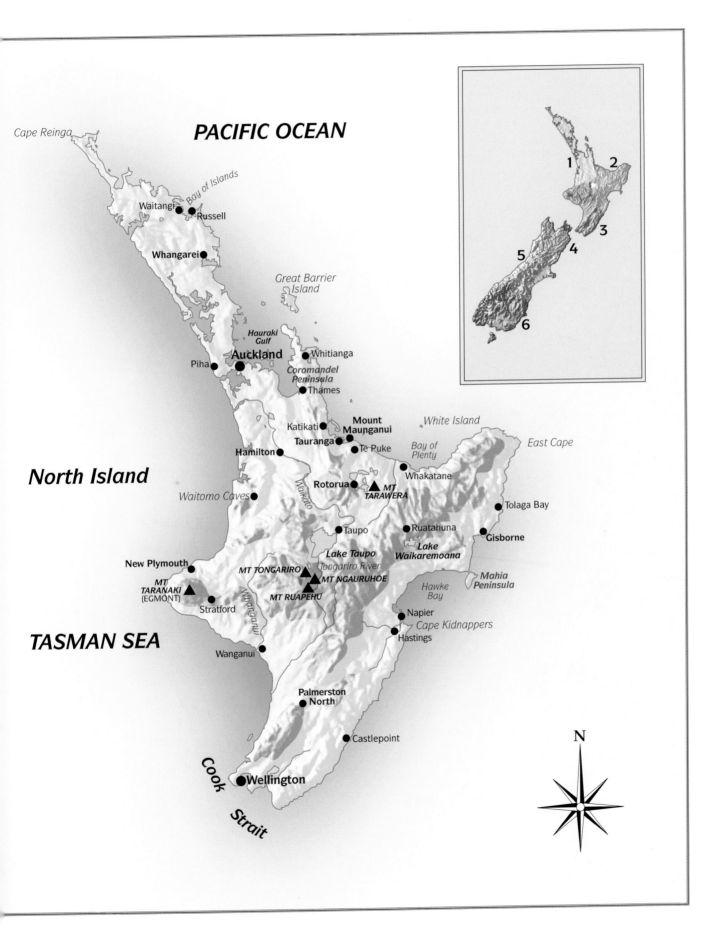

PACIFIC OCEAN

Cape Reinga

Bay of Islands

Waitangi
Russell

Whangarei

Great Barrier
Island

Hauraki
Gulf

Piha
Auckland
Whitianga

Coromandel
Peninsula
Thames

Katikati
Mount
Maunganui
Tauranga
Te Puke

Hamilton

White Island

Bay of
Plenty

East Cape

North Island

Waitomo Caves

Waikato

Rotorua
MT
TARAWERA

Whakatane

Tolaga Bay

Taupo

Ruatahuna

Lake
Waikaremoana

Gisborne

Lake Taupo

New Plymouth

MT TONGARIRO

Tongariro River

MT
TARANAKI
(EGMONT)

MT NGAURUHOE

MT RUAPEHU

Mahia
Peninsula

Hawke
Bay

TASMAN SEA

Stratford

Whanganui

Napier
Cape Kidnappers
Hastings

Wanganui

Palmerston
North

Castlepoint

Cook
Strait

Wellington

N

1
2

3

5
4

6

PROFILE OF NEW ZEALAND

Rising in parts over three and a half kilometres (two miles) above the Pacific Ocean, the two major islands that make up New Zealand describe a slender 1600km (995-mile) arc thrust up from the ocean floor by the collision of major tectonic plates and violent volcanic action. This lonely land, surrounded by only a few small islands and situated 2000km (1200 miles) from the nearest major landmass, was one of the last to be settled by humans when the Moa-hunters arrived in the ninth century.

This isolation, combined with an extraordinary diversity of environments – ranging from alpine peaks, lakes and glaciers, to volcanic landscapes, dramatic fiords, rainforests, grassy plains and golden beaches – has led to the development of a unique fauna and flora. New Zealand is the preserve of birds, from the Giant Moa, an extinct flightless bird which grew over three metres (10ft) tall; to the Kea, a cheeky alpine parrot; the rare Yellow-eyed Penguin; and the secretive national emblem, the kiwi. With the exception of two native bats, all of the many land mammals which now inhabit the islands were imported by the intrepid Polynesian and later European and Asian settlers who made this land their own.

The Maori settled in New Zealand in the 14th century, and named it Aotearoa (land of the long white cloud). Captain James Cook was the first European to land on New Zealand in 1769, but Europeans only settled on the islands in the 19th century. The Maori named them pakeha, a name still in common use today. Gradually, despite territorial wars and colonial influences, a distinct national identity has emerged from the many cultures of the pioneering peoples who travelled to this distant land. The nearly four million people who now live in New Zealand pride themselves on being 'Kiwis', a collective term for a nation characterized by a spirit of innovation, ingenuity and fierce independence.

THE LAND

Surrounded by great expanses of ocean, New Zealand exists because of a major fault in the earth's crust between the Pacific and Indian tectonic plates. The fault's most obvious feature is the Southern Alps mountain range, running virtually the length of the South Island and rising to over three and a half kilometres (two miles) above sea level. The North Island also has a series of near-continuous parallel ranges running from Wellington in the south to the East Cape in the east. The forces that created New Zealand are still at work. Parts of the Southern Alps continue to be uplifted at around 10mm (0.4in) a year – a small rate in human terms but quite fast in the context of geological time. In the central regions of the North Island lesser faults have created magnificent volcanic landscapes. Mt Ruapehu, the North Island's highest mountain, is an active volcano that has erupted several times in recent years, spitting out ash, steam and mud.

New Zealand's southerly position on the globe (its main islands lie between latitudes 34 and 47 degrees south) has led to ice in the form of glaciers, which have also played a large part in sculpting the landscape.

Together the forces of ice, volcanoes, highly pressured faults, as well as erosion, have created a landscape that is not only spectacular, but which is also extraordinarily diverse.

THE SOUTH

Arguably New Zealand's most imposing natural feature is the Southern Alps. Often referred to as the backbone of the South Island, the Alps run for approximately 700km (430 miles) along the length of the island, and are often referred to as the Main Divide. Very few roads cross the Alps, and to cross over between Mt Cook village and Fox Glacier township on the West Coast (a straight-

Page 8: *Sperm Whale off Kaikoura.*
Page 9: *Maori carving, Otago Museum.*
Above: *Hooker River footbridge and Mt Sefton, Mount Cook National Park.*
Left: *The Grand Chateau, with Mt Ruapehu in the background.*

line distance of less than 30km; 18 miles), vehicles have to divert via Haast Pass in the south (nearly 500km; 310 miles) or Arthur's Pass to the north (nearly 700km; 430 miles). It is this central section of the Alps that is most impressive, with over 100 peaks higher than 2400m (7800ft), culminating in Mt Cook at 3754m (12,316ft). One of Mt Cook's Maori names, Aorangi, is translated as 'cloud piercer' – an apt name for the tallest peak in this rugged region.

Much of the Southern Alps is permanently covered in snow as, despite New Zealand's temperate climate, annual snowfall is greater than the rate of melt at high altitude. The build-up of snow compresses lower layers into ice, thereby forming glaciers. There are more than 360 glaciers in the Southern Alps, with the largest, Tasman Glacier (near Mt Cook), measuring 29km (18 miles) in length and up to 3km (1.8 miles) in width at some points. Far from being static, glaciers are continually on the move, some by just a few centimetres a day and others by as much as several metres.

Sheep are often seen being driven along rural New Zealand roads, as here on the road to Mt Cook, in the Southern Alps, central South Island.

Day hikers are guided up Fox Glacier, in Westland, in the South Island.

Westland

To the west of the Alps is Westland, an area usually known simply as the West Coast. With a small population and large tracts of land in a natural state, the West Coast has a 'frontier' feel about it. A distinct region of New Zealand, it is known specifically for its lush rainforests, wild weather, and its hardened locals. Nestled on a narrow strip between the Tasman Sea and the Southern Alps, it is a trap for rain clouds brought in by the prevailing westerly winds and stopped by the mountains. With snowy mountain peaks close to the sea (Mt Cook is just 30km, or 18 miles, from the Tasman Sea), glaciers flow down to well within 20km (12 miles) of the coast at Fox and Franz Josef – a characteristic that is unusual away from the poles. This, combined with the easy accessibility of the two glaciers, makes them popular with sightseers and tourists.

It is thought that in an earlier ice age, glaciers completely covered most of the central West Coast, wiping out the beech forest that still dominates areas north and south of here. This explains a belt of quicker rejuvenating podocarp forest in the region where the ice receded, but the almost complete lack of slower spreading beech forest.

Southland
Fiordland

While Westland may have a wild feel to it, Fiordland, further south along the same coast, has a distinctly primeval atmosphere. As its name implies, huge fiords indent its coastline – more remnants of an ice age when glaciers carved spectacular furrows in the earth's surface. The area is largely uninhabited, with the majority of Fiordland being encompassed in the 1.2 million-hectare (2.9 million-acre) Fiordland National Park, itself part of the 2.6 million-hectare (6.4 million-acre) South-West New Zealand World Heritage Area. This latter area is also known as Te Wahipounamu ('the place of greenstone'), and covers other protected areas including Mt Cook, Westland and Mt Aspiring national parks, and contains over 1000km (620 miles) of largely inaccessible coastline.

The most famous of all the fiords is Milford Sound. Here Mitre Peak rises steeply from the water, soaring skyward for over a mile (1695m; 5561ft), and resembling the improbable mountains a child might draw. Hemmed in by sheer cliff faces rising far above its waters, the 16km-long (10-mile) sound is one of New Zealand's most dramatic landscapes.

Fiordland also has several lakes, including New Zealand's second largest, Lake Te Anau. Many of the region's lakes are in glacial valleys, offering beautiful reflections of the surrounding mountains.

One part of this rugged region that does get a number of regular hikers is the Milford Track, famous for its magnificent mountains, sheer cliffs, hanging valleys, canyons and waterfalls. The driver's equivalent of the Milford Track, the Milford Road World Heritage Highway is one of Fiordland's few roads, and winds its way along U-shaped glacial valleys, dwarfed by steep walls rising to snow-capped peaks far above.

Stewart Island

Equally inaccessible is Stewart Island, 30km (18 miles) south of mainland New Zealand. From its only settlement at Halfmoon Bay, it is not possible to travel more than around 4km (2.5 miles) by road. However there are around 250km (155 miles) of walking tracks on the island, or alternatively boats can access much of the island's 750km (460 miles) of coastline. Like Fiordland, very little of Stewart Island has been affected by humans, and its wildlife, namely birds,

The Otago Peninsula shelters Otago Harbour, and is a haven for rare species of wildlife.

has not suffered the devastation caused to mainland cousins by introduced mustelids – ferrets, stoats and weasels. As a result, bird life is abundant and there are places on the island where even kiwis are seen in the wild on a regular basis – probably the only place in the country where this happens.

The island's Maori name Rakiura means 'glowing sky', and refers to the spectacular sunsets experienced in summer at latitudes this far south. Many of Stewart Island's European names are also evocative, and include Port Adventure, Hellfire and Smugglers Cove.

Stewart Island and Fiordland are both part of the province of Southland. Away from these two rugged areas, much of Southland is flat fertile farmland, moving into green pastures on rolling hills nearer the province of Otago to the north west.

Otago

Otago and Southland share the region of the Catlins – an almost forgotten but nevertheless scenically beautiful area on the coast, well away from the main north-south road. This sparsely populated district is predominantly covered in lowland forest that hides many

waterfalls, rivers and streams. Lagoons empty onto deserted golden beaches where wildlife is common. Nugget Point has colonies of New Zealand Fur Seals and the rare Yellow-eyed Penguin.

Further north the rest of coastal Otago is characterized by alternating beaches and headlands, the most prominent feature of which is the 25km-long (15-mile) Otago Peninsula, which shelters Otago Harbour. With colonies of albatrosses, New Zealand Fur Seals, and Little Blue and Yellow-eyed penguins, the peninsula lays claim to being New Zealand's wildlife capital.

Inland, in the centre of the southern South Island, Central Otago is a region of dramatically varied landscapes. Snowy peaks overlook a series of beautiful lakes, and several rivers – including the Shotover and Kawarau – have cut deep gorges and canyons. Both of these rivers help feed the 338km (210-mile) Clutha River, helping to give it the greatest flow of any in the country. While the topography of some of the region is steep and mountainous, other areas have wide flat valleys and high rolling hills covered in tussock. Much of the region is very barren, with little or no

Sea kayaks are an ideal way to explore Stewart Island. With virtually no roads, all transport is by water, or on foot.

native bush, but the wide open spaces have a stark beauty of their own.

In summer the region has some of the country's hottest temperatures, often above 30°C (86°F). At this time of year Central Otago's lakes, rivers, mountains and hills become a giant playground for holidaymakers, tourists and locals.

In winter, however, it is one of New Zealand's coldest areas. Hoarfrosts occur in some valleys where freezing fog and mist obliterate the sun for days on end, keeping temperatures below zero. Frost builds up on trees, powerlines, fences and grass creating a beautiful white wonderland, albeit in temperatures inhospitable to humans.

In winter the region also becomes an ideal playground for winter sports, including ice skating and curling, but in particular skiing at several wonderfully scenic ski fields near the resort towns of Wanaka and Queenstown.

Mackenzie Country

The Lindis Pass road travels through fold upon fold of tussock-carpeted hills, and separates Central Otago from the Mackenzie Country. The lakes and open tussock lands of the Mackenzie Country are never far from the majestic backdrop of the Southern Alps. These moun-

tains provide the water for the region's lakes and rivers, often coloured grey-green by fine particles of rock that have been crushed by glaciers. This continual supply of water has been harnessed here by means of a series of canals and dams, and also further downstream in the Waitaki Valley, providing a large portion of the country's hydro-electricity. With its close proximity to the Alps, the Mackenzie Country also suffers harsh winters, but this is compensated for by ski fields and impressive winter scenery.

Canterbury

Also under the ever-present Southern Alps, but further to the north, are the Canterbury Plains. The contrast between the country's steepest, highest region and its largest flat area could hardly be more complete. Fertile green pastures and golden wheatfields have replaced the original tussock lands, forming a patchwork of colours over this vast plain. Fields are separated by long straight fences and roads, and rows of trees provide shelter from the strong winds that come from the mountains. At regular intervals rivers flowing from the mountains reach the plain and spread out over wide gravel beds up to several kilometres across, forming a myriad braided streams.

On the Canterbury coast, jutting out from an otherwise regular coastline, is Banks Peninsula. The peninsula rises high above the plain that it adjoins, deceiving Captain Cook into charting it as an island in 1770. At the time it was in fact only connected to the mainland by swamps. Originally two large volcanoes, the peninsula has eroded away to just half its original height, but it retains a steep and irregular shoreline, with many sheltered bays and two large harbours, Akaroa and Lyttelton. They are thought to be the remnants of the two ancient craters, now eroded and connected to the sea. Banks Peninsula has its own distinct climate – far milder than the frosty winters and hot dry summers of much of the Canterbury Plains, and resulting in quite different vegetation, including palm trees.

Marlborough

Further up the South Island's east coast in southern Marlborough are the Kaikoura Ranges. The Seaward Kaikouras look spectacular in winter as their snow-covered peaks drop from a height of up to 2600m (8500ft), straight into the Pacific Ocean. The main north–south highway is here squeezed between the mountains and sea, sometimes forced

Caravans span out on the Canterbury Plains near Lake Coleridge, which offers excellent trout and salmon fishing to holidaymakers.

Negotiating steep tracks which rise above the city, Wellington's cable car offers passengers superb scenic views across the city skyline.

THE NORTH
Wellington

Wellington itself is on a fault line, and its harbour – like several of the country's large natural harbours – is the remnant of an ancient volcanic crater.

Cook Strait provides a relatively narrow but often formidable barrier between the North and South islands. As the only real break between the mountains running the length of the South Island and the chain of ranges on the North Island, the strait is notorious for its rough seas and very strong winds – a climatic trait that also dogs Wellington.

Taranaki

In Taranaki, in the west, the classic snow-capped volcanic shape of Mt Taranaki (2518m; 8261ft) dominates the region. The mountain became protected in 1900 when it became the focus of the circular Egmont National Park. Mt Egmont, as it was then known, had its original Maori name, Taranaki, officially reinstated in 1986, and is today known by both names.

Dozens of rivers and streams flow off the mountain in every direction, to a ring of fertile plains below. These plains support a strong dairy industry, but in recent decades new resources have been discovered in Taranaki – natural gas and oil exist in commercial quantities beneath the land and off the coast.

Volcanic Plateau

Just 22km (13 miles) separate the North Island from the South Island, but the landscape on each is quite different. While the Southern Alps have resulted from upliftment caused by two continental plates pushing into one another, many of the North Island's major features are volcanic in origin.

through tunnels at headlands. Parallel to the Seaward Kaikouras are the Inland Kaikouras, separated by a fault down which the Clarence River runs.

The Marlborough Sounds consist of a maze of inlets, sounds, coves and islands. They were created when the sea level rose after the last ice age, flooding numerous river valleys. In this largely unspoilt region, which has few roads, boats are the main form of transport. It is through the sounds that the inter-island ferries travel, linking the North and South islands. The ferries wind their way for 35km (21 miles) along Tory Channel and Queen Charlotte Sound. Pelorus Sound is, however, the largest waterway in the sounds. At around 50km (31 miles) long, it has over 300km (190 miles) of coast with its various arms and inlets.

Nelson

Like Marlborough, the Nelson region to the west (whose main town is called Nelson) has a reputation for being warm and sunny, making the very large Tasman Bay and Golden Bay popular with holidaymakers in the summer. On the edge of Tasman Bay is Abel Tasman National Park, renowned for its golden sandy beaches and coves of clear aquamarine waters, all fringed by native forests. Also in the region are Nelson Lakes National Park and a recent addition to the New Zealand parks system, Kahurangi National Park, which stretches across to the West Coast. Nearby the northernmost feature of the South Island is Cape Farewell, and an adjoining sand spit called Farewell Spit that juts out 25km (15 miles) into the sea.

The Motunui plant near New Plymouth is the only one in the world that can produce both petrol and methanol from natural gas, which is one of Taranaki's major resources.

ash hundreds of metres into the sky. At 2797m (9176ft) it is the North Island's highest mountain, substantially higher than Mt Ngauruhoe (2290m; 7516ft) and Mt Tongariro (1968m; 6457ft). All three volcanoes are contained within Tongariro National Park, established in 1887 as New Zealand's first national park.

The park is a catchment area for the North Island's second longest river, the Whanganui, which travels 290km (180 miles) before discharging into the Tasman Sea. The park also indirectly feeds the country's longest river, the 425km-long (264-mile) Waikato. The Tongariro River flows from the park into the southern region of Lake Taupo. At its northern end this lake is drained by the Waikato, which after just 8km (5 miles) plunges over the spectacular Huka Falls.

Lake Taupo, like the nearby mountains, is of volcanic origin. Less than 2000 years ago a massive volcanic explosion blew debris over an area of 7000km^2 (2702 sq. miles), leaving a huge crater which filled with water to create the 606km^2 (233-sq.-mile) lake.

Dominating the centre of the island are three volcanoes, Mounts Ruapehu, Ngauruhoe, and Tongariro, and Lake Taupo, the country's largest lake. All three volcanoes are active, and emit steam and ash from time to time, occasionally with great violence. In recent times Mt Ruapehu has erupted dramatically, sending mud and

Near its source of Lake Taupo, New Zealand's longest river, the Waikato, is forced into a narrow gorge culminating in Huka Falls.

The lake is now better known for recreational pursuits, and is particularly famous for its trout fishing.

Nearby thermal power stations use highly pressurized steam from very hot underground water sources to produce electricity. It is one of the few places where humans have managed to control the North Island's thermal activity. More often nature's forces dominate, occasionally with disastrous consequences. On Christmas eve in 1953 an enormous mud slide cascaded down the mountain from Mt Ruapehu's crater lake. It wiped out a railway bridge, and with it a passenger train, killing 151 people in what became known as the Tangiwai Rail Disaster.

A similar number of people were killed when Mt Tarawera, to the north of Lake Taupo, erupted in 1886. The eruption also destroyed world-famous pink and white terraces formed over thousands of years by the silica residue from a geyser. Mount Tarawera is part of an area of concentrated volcanic activity around Rotorua. Numerous lakes in the region provide an ingredient that, when combined with this volcanic activity, produces geysers. This region is one of only three main areas on the globe where this happens (the others are in the USA and Iceland). At Whakarewarewa, geysers

regularly shoot strong jets of hot water up to 30m (98ft) into the air. Nearby, boiling pools of mud bubble away and within a few hundred metres there are over 500 hot springs. The thermal activity in the Rotorua region is part of the volcanic belt that runs from Mt Ruapehu in the south, north to the regularly steaming White Island, 50km (31 miles) from the coast in the Bay of Plenty.

Hawke's Bay
The region of Hawke's Bay is situated around the long curving coastline of Hawke Bay, which runs from the 20km-long (12-mile) Mahia Peninsula in the north to Cape Kidnappers in the south. In season it is home to a colony of thousands of gannets.

South of Hawke Bay, the coast runs in a southwesterly direction, roughly parallel to the inland ranges of Ruahine, Tararua and Rimutaka. These ranges are part of a chain that starts in the East Cape and runs almost continuously along a fault line to Wellington at the southern extremity of the North Island.

East Cape
North of Hawke's Bay the regions of Poverty Bay and the East Cape have been less suitable for economic exploitation, due largely to isolation and land suit-

Above: *Waiotapu is one of several places near Rotorua where the pressure from superheated underground water explodes from the surface as a geyser.*
Below: *Cape Kidnappers' gannet colony.*

ability. The Raukumara Ranges form the backbone of the East Cape, leaving little flat land and isolating the settlements dotted around the coastline. The region is one of the least affected by outside influence, and the small quiet coastal

communities composed of predominantly Maori people are considered by many to be the 'real' New Zealand.

A glimpse of what New Zealand was like before the coming of humans can be seen further south at Urewera National Park. This steep and rugged park contains the North Island's largest untouched area of native forest, as well as the beautiful Lake Waikaremoana.

Bay of Plenty

Fertile land and a pleasant climate have given the Bay of Plenty region a reputation that matches the name given to it by Captain Cook, particularly when it comes to forestry, Kiwifruit and agriculture. Long sweeping beaches separated by headlands stretch from Cape Runaway in the east to the Coromandel Peninsula in the west.

King Country and Waikato
King Country

In the King Country, just south of Waikato, are the Waitomo Caves. Around 100km (62 miles) of the limestone caves have been explored to date, and it is thought there may be at least as much still to be explored. The network of caves features cathedral-like caverns, huge vertical shafts, underground rivers and lakes, glow-worm grottoes, stalactites and stalagmites – much of which can be visited on guided tours by foot or boat, or for the more adventurous, by abseiling, caving and black-water rafting.

Western Waikato

The Waikato region is famed for its fertile plains, which support a large number of dairy cows. The plains are largely built up by pumice and ash deposits originally from the volcanic explosion which created Lake Taupo. The region, through which the Waikato River flows, also has

The eastern extremity of Northland's maritime playground, the Bay of Islands, is marked by the jagged coastline of Cape Brett.

large coal deposits which provide energy for a large power station at Huntly.

Coromandel

The beautiful Coromandel Peninsula is known for its bays, steep hills and valleys, and its native forests. While its beauty and low population have drawn people to the area, its minerals and in earlier days its Kauri trees have also drawn companies who wish to exploit the local resources. This has often led to disputes over land usage in this region.

Northland

At Auckland a narrow isthmus of not much more than a kilometre (0.6 of a mile) across links the King Country and Waikato to the northernmost 330km (205 miles) of the North Island. Because of its northerly situation, the Northland region has mild winters, warm humid summers, and a relatively high rainfall as a result of being sandwiched between the Pacific Ocean and Tasman Sea.

This long, slender piece of land also has a very irregular coastline in places. The 65km-long (40-mile) Kaipara Harbour on Northland's west coast has many arms and inlets and, like the South Island's Marlborough Sounds, is a drowned river system, as is Hokianga Harbour to the north. Near Hokianga are forest parks that hold remnants of Northland's great Kauri forests, including some giant trees up to 2000 years old. Not far away on the east coast of Northland, the Bay of Islands is another drowned river system.

The Bay of Islands was the scene of some of the earliest European settlement in New Zealand, but more recently has become known for excellent deep-sea fishing around its 150 or so islands.

Ninety Mile Beach has a far less complicated coastline, which is very nearly straight for much of its 96km (60-mile) length. The deserted beach is away from major towns or roads, and stretches northwest towards Cape Reinga, often considered to be the northernmost tip of New Zealand. 'Cape Reinga to the Bluff' is a term commonly used to encompass the whole of mainland New Zealand. However, these two sites are not the northern- and southernmost points, which are in fact Surville Cliffs near North Cape, and Slope Point in the Catlins, respectively.

Offshore Territories

In addition to the two main islands (referred to collectively as the 'mainland') and Stewart Island, New Zealand has many offshore islands. Subantarctic islands far to the south of the mainland include the Snares, Auckland Islands and the Campbell Islands, while in an easterly direction lie the Antipodes, Bounty and Chatham islands. Several hundred people live on the Chatham Islands but most of the other southern isles are home only to wildlife including albatrosses, penguins and seals, and the occasional hardy scientific researcher.

Other New Zealand island territories include the Kermadecs, nearly 1000km (621 miles) to the north, and the country is also responsible for the Tokelaus, a small group of atolls within 10 degrees of the equator and more than 3000km (1864 miles) north of mainland New Zealand.

The other major offshore territory is Ross Dependency in Antarctica, where there are permanent scientific headquarters at Scott Base.

CLIMATE

Because of the mountainous nature of much of New Zealand, weather patterns can be extremely varied, even between areas of close proximity. Milford Sound can receive over 6000mm (236in) of rain per year, yet Alexandra in Central Otago, less than 150km (90 miles) away, may receive barely one-twentieth of that amount. In general, the eastern areas are drier – some are even drought prone – while the western areas receive high rainfall. This is particularly true where there are high mountains, which block the prevailing westerly rain clouds, and cause a rain shadow to the east. Unlike the tropics, New Zealand has no real rainy season, with most areas receiving rain throughout the year.

Temperatures can also vary a great deal, and some of the hottest places in summer are some of the coldest in winter. This is particularly true of places away from the sea like the central North Island and inland Otago and Canterbury in the South Island, where temperatures above 30°C (86°F) are common in summer, while winter days can be close to freezing. Generally the north is warmer than the south, but regional topography and daily weather patterns have more influence on climate than latitude does. On average, the maximum daily temperature of Auckland city in the north is just four degrees warmer than Dunedin in the south.

FAUNA AND FLORA

A peculiarity of the list of New Zealand fauna is the almost complete lack of mammals, at least on land. Since the separation of New Zealand from Gondwana around 80 million years ago, the country has been isolated from other landmasses. This lack of any serious predators has led to the evolution of many unusual creatures, in particular flightless birds.

In the same way, isolation has led to the evolution of new and unique species of flora, or the continuation of ancient species that have died out elsewhere. Of around 2000 native plant species of all types, around three-quarters are found nowhere else.

FAUNA
Land Mammals

Land mammals never evolved in New Zealand. The only native mammals are two species of bat, the Long-tailed and

A visitor is dwarfed by huge crevasses near the top of New Zealand's longest glacier, the 29km (18-mile) Tasman Glacier.

Marine Mammals

While native land mammals are scarce, New Zealand's fish-rich waters are home to an abundant variety of marine mammals. Various species of whales, dolphins and seals are regularly spotted around the coastline.

Few people would fail to be impressed by a close encounter with a 20m-long (65ft), 50-tonne male Sperm Whale. Far from being just a once-in-a-lifetime experience, these huge mammals may be seen several times a day off the South Island's Pacific coast at Kaikoura. After diving to massive depths (they have been tracked to over 2000m, or 6562ft, below the surface) for approximately 45 minutes, they spend a few minutes on the surface to re-oxygenate. Then, signalling another dive, water pours off their huge tail flukes as they raise them spectacularly into the air. Sperm Whales are the largest member of the Odontoceti – the family of toothed whales and dolphins.

the Short-tailed bat. However, there are many wild introduced mammals. These include rabbits and several species of deer, which were initially introduced for sport hunting. Both have at times reached population levels that have caused severe environment degradation, making expensive control programmes necessary.

Predators like ferrets, stoats, and weasels were introduced to control the rabbits – but ever since have taken a severe toll on native birds, many of which are defenceless as they evolved without predators. Likewise, rats and cats have also had a severe impact on native birds.

Another introduction that has been disastrous for New Zealand's flora and fauna has been the Possum, introduced for its fur. It has now reached such large population levels that it is devastating vast tracts of native forest. Hares, goats, pigs, Chamois from Europe, Tahr from the Himalayas, and wallabies from Australia have also been introduced, some of which have also had to be controlled.

Above: *The huge tail fluke of a Sperm Whale lifts out of the water as it dives to feed in the ocean depths.*
Below: *The New Zealand Fur Seal occurs in many colonies around the South Island.*

The smallest member of the Odontoceti can be found alongside the Sperm Whale at Kaikoura. The 1.5m-long (5ft) Hector's Dolphin is the world's smallest dolphin, and is also thought to be the world's rarest. It is found only in New Zealand waters, mainly around the

The beautiful Kotuku, or White Heron.

South Island. Other dolphins like the Dusky, Common and Bottlenose species – along with Pilot, Southern Right, and Orca (or Killer) Whales – are among 34 dolphin and whale species that have been sighted in New Zealand waters.

Leopard Seals occasionally travel north from the Antarctic region to visit New Zealand. Elephant Seals, named for their large protruding snouts, sometimes land on the coast, although most of their time is spent at sea and in breeding grounds to the south of the mainland. Hooker's Sea Lions, unique to the region, are also occasionally seen. By far the most common type of seal on the coast of the mainland is the New Zealand Fur Seal.

Birds

New Zealand has been home to some very unusual birds. Best known is the now-extinct Giant Moa, a massive 3–4m (10–13ft) tall flightless bird. Although

there were more than 20 different species of moa (not all were huge – some were under 1m, or 3ft, tall), all became extinct by the time of the arrival of the Europeans. Other long extinct New Zealand birds include the massive Haast's Giant Eagle, which was said to be capable of killing a human, and a giant penguin as tall as a person.

Although the birds occurring in New Zealand today tend not to have the bright colours of some of the exotic birds of South America, Africa or Australia, there are nevertheless some unique and strange species.

The best known New Zealand bird is the kiwi, a flightless nocturnal bird roughly the size of a chicken (see page 65). The bird's name, which comes from its call, has perhaps become more famous than the bird itself. 'Kiwi' has been used for Kiwifruit, several product brand names, and sports teams. It is also used to refer to the people of New Zealand collectively, probably more so than the term 'New Zealander'.

Kiwis live in dense bush and forests, and this – combined with their nocturnal habits and threatened status – means that it is very difficult to find them in their natural habitats. With the very unusual feature of nostrils at the tip of its long bill, the kiwi is perfectly adapted to hunt for worms and underground insects. It can also rake up the ground with its strong legs and claws – tools that double as a formidable defence in an adult bird.

With the arrival of humans came a number of predators that New Zealand's bird species were not adapted to cope with. Many of these birds are now extremely endangered, like the ground-dwelling Kakapo – a huge (the world's largest) green nocturnal parrot. Although the Kakapo can glide from a high to a low place, it has lost the ability to fly properly. Kakapo have been moved to islands like Codfish near Stewart Island where there are no known predators and a breeding programme has been set up. Even with this extra help Kakapo

A ranger checks a Royal Albatross at Taiaroa Head Albatross Colony.

numbers are very low (around 53 known birds), and often several years go by without a single new chick being hatched.

Another very rare flightless bird is the Takahe. The 60cm-tall (2ft) Takahe is bright blue with a green back and a large red bill, and was thought to be extinct after 1898 until a population was discovered near Te Anau in 1948. Even with full protection, removal to safe breeding grounds and captive breeding programmes, the Takahe is still very rare with less than 200 birds in existence.

Very similar looking but slightly smaller, the Pukeko (sometimes called a Swamp Hen), is much more common. It is most often seen wading through marshes and wet swampy areas, although it can fly. About the same size, and also in the rail family is the flightless Weka, or Wood-hen, which has plumage in varying shades of brown to black. It has become infamous for its bold thefts, not only of campers' food, but also of shiny objects like pocket knives, watches and jewellery.

Also known for its cheeky character is an unusual indigenous parrot, the Kea. As the world's only alpine parrot, the Kea is commonly seen at sites like ski-fields and at the West Coast glaciers. Keas have become used to humans, and often destroy the rubber door and

The Yellow-eyed Penguin, the world's rarest penguin, nests on the coast of the South Island.

window seals on cars, and bindings on unattended skis – in fact anything that they find curious and can rip at with their strong sharp beaks. Their clown-like nature has endeared them to many, and as they now number just a few thousand they are officially protected – although not everyone agrees with this. Farmers once shot them as pests as they have been known to attack lambs, and their destructive habits cost car rental companies tens of thousands of dollars in repair bills every year.

The Kakapo, the Kea and the Kaka are New Zealand's three indigenous parrots. The Kaka, while similar looking to the Kea, lives in native forests rather than above the tree- or snowline in the alpine areas.

New Zealand and the surrounding islands are also home to several species of an aquatic flightless bird found only in the southern hemisphere, the penguin.

The most common species on the two main islands is the Little Blue Penguin, which at just 40cm (15in) long is the world's smallest penguin. It nests at sites around the South Island and in the lower North Island, but as it spends the day at sea and only returns to land after dark, it is difficult to see.

Fiordland Crested Penguins vie with Yellow-eyed species for the title of 'world's rarest penguin'. They nest around the southern coast of the South Island, a region which also gets occasional visits from other types of crested penguins.

Despite being labelled 'the rarest', the Yellow-eyed Penguin is one of the easiest to see, at nesting sites along the southeast coast of the South Island. At a nesting site on Otago Peninsula, just half an hour's drive from the city of Dunedin, visitors can view these penguins at close range. Just a few kilometres away is the nesting site for what is perhaps the

greatest flying bird of all – the Royal Albatross. Taiaroa Head at the tip of Otago Peninsula is the only mainland breeding site in the world for albatrosses, with others using the remote and inaccessible islands of the Southern Ocean.

New Zealand's offshore islands are breeding grounds for many species of albatross, and the country's coastal waters also see a variety of other sea birds. These include many species of petrel, cormorants (known locally as 'shags'), and shearwaters. The Sooty Shearwater (or 'Muttonbird') is found in large numbers near Stewart Island, and is harvested by Maori.

Also found in vast numbers at their colony at Cape Kidnappers on the east coast of the North Island are Australasian Gannets. A familiar sight in many coastal areas is the White-faced Heron, while its cousin, the White Heron, or Kotuku, is rare in New Zealand. Although numerous in other parts of the world, the White Heron has just one breeding ground on the west coast of the South Island. It has become a symbol of rare beauty, largely because there are not many more than 100 birds in the country.

Found in similarly low numbers in New Zealand, but much more widespread elsewhere, are Royal Spoonbills. Smaller waders range from common species of oystercatcher and stilt, to very rare and endangered birds like the Black Stilt, which numbers less than 100 individuals.

More generally seen are some of New Zealand's well-known forest species, many of which come to feed in suburban areas when conditions are right. The large Native Pigeon, sometimes called Wood Pigeon, or Kereru, is often seen gorging itself in fruit trees until it is so full it has difficulty flying. Even in normal conditions it has a distinct laboured wingbeat – a loud whooping sound as if the bird is struggling to take off.

Although not scarce, the Bellbird's distinct song is heard much more than the bird is seen. A clear tinkling bell sound with an almost crystal quality is its trademark, although this can be confused with the call of the Tui, which seems to mimic the Bellbird as part of its variety of song. Also known for its call, and named for the sound it makes, is the 'Morepork', a native owl.

Reptiles and Amphibians

Millions of years of independent evolution have left New Zealand with some unique reptiles and amphibians. Some, like the Tuatara, are unique because they haven't evolved, remaining the same as they were in the time of the dinosaurs. The Tuatara is the only surviving species of the Rhynchocephalia order, the rest of which died out 100 million years ago in the Jurassic period. Although it looks like a lizard, it actually forms its own reptile family, separate from turtles, crocodiles, snakes and lizards. Taking nine or 10 months to lay an egg, a further 15 months for it to hatch, 20 years to reach maturity and 60 years to be fully grown, the Tuatara – in keeping with its ancient beginnings – is a very slow developer. It grows up to 60cm (2ft) long. 'Tuatara' refers to the row of erect spiny scales on its back, meaning 'line of spears'.

In the lizard family there are around 40 native species of gecko and skink. Indigenous geckos are unusual in that they give birth to live young instead of laying eggs. Apart from Tuatara and

Mount Aspiring towers above a fly-fisherman trying his luck for trout in Lake Wanaka.

The Tuatara grows to 60cm (2ft) long.

some lizards, New Zealand has no other reptiles and is one of the few countries of the world that doesn't have snakes. In fact there are no animals that pose any real threat to humans.

In addition to introduced frogs, which are widespread across the country, there are three native species: Hamilton's, Archey's and Hochstetter's frogs. Compared to most frogs, they have some primitive features (they miss the tadpole stage and lack eardrums).

Insects

There are just two poisonous spiders in New Zealand, the Katipo and the related Red-back, and bites from either

are extremely rare. However, antivenin is available to negate the effects.

Many of New Zealand's insects, like many native birds, have lost the ability to fly. Several species of flightless grasshopper exist, including the Giant Weta which can have a body length of up to 100mm (4in). Glow-worms are fairly common, but are most famously found in their thousands in the Waitomo Caves, where their flashing lights (luring flying insects into their silky thread traps) are an impressive sight.

Fish

Dominating New Zealand's rivers and lakes are introduced species of fish like Brown and Rainbow trout, and salmon, found in numbers that attract anglers from around the world. Whitebait, a New

Zealand delicacy, are the young of a native fish (*Galaxias*) and are caught by the thousand in nets, mainly near river mouths, especially on the South Island's West Coast. Anglers also come for marlin and other big-game fish found in northern coastal waters. The sea provides large catches of many different species including tuna, hoki, snapper, dory, cod, and squid. New Zealand's waters are also home to commercially harvested shellfish like oysters, mussels, scallops, paua (related to abalone), and crayfish.

FLORA

Dominating New Zealand's flora are the great trees of the forests, which before the arrival of humans covered up to 80

Top: *The Mount Cook Lily.*
Above: *New Zealand is probably better endowed with ferns than is any other temperate country.*

percent of the country. The forests can be divided into three major types, by species: podocarp and beech forests are found on both the South and North islands, while in the north of the North Island are the Kauri forests.

The podocarp forests are made up of 17 different species of tree which, like the Kauri, are conifers. These ancient trees were dominant before flowering plants spread across the planet. Podocarp species, including Rimu and Totara, are sought after for timber, though in most areas they are protected from felling. Both species can grow to more than a thousand years old and over 30m (100ft) tall; this made Totara a popular tree for large Maori war canoes in earlier times. Other podocarps, Matai and Miro, grow nearly as tall, while Kahekateas have been known to reach 60m (200ft).

While podocarp forests occur in the North Island and on the west coast of the South Island, beech forests dominate the northwest and southwest of the South Island, and can also be found in parts of the North Island. The five New Zealand species of beech tree can grow to around 30m (150ft) tall.

The Kauri tree, a conifer, can grow to over 50m (164ft) tall and over 20m (65ft) around the base. Some of these trees are up to 2000 years old. Although now largely protected, Kauri wood is a fine timber, characterized by a straight, uniformly sized trunk which is branchless until very high up in the tree. Its gum was sought after by the early settlers for use in paints, polishes and varnish.

Commonly seen throughout both islands are Manuka and the very similar but larger Kanuka. Both are known as Tea Trees because of the tea-like drink brewed from their leaves by early settlers.

The Pohutukawa, or New Zealand Christmas Tree, which has a covering of bright red flowers around Christmas time, occurs naturally in coastal areas of the North Island, although it has been cultivated across the country. The similar and related Rata also has a profuse covering of bright red flowers in summer,

Some of the country's most pristine ancient Kauri forest is protected in Waipoua Forest in Northland.

and while the southern species grows as a tree to around 15m (50ft), the northern species starts on a host tree, sending its roots down and eventually growing around and killing the original host, to attain a height of up to 25m (80ft).

Another tree with bright flowers is the Kowhai. The golden-yellow bell-shaped flowers on this relatively common tree are a national symbol.

The Silver Fern, one of 10 New Zealand tree ferns, is another national symbol. The silvery underside of the fronds serve as the emblem for the national rugby team, the All Blacks, and the national netball team is called the Silver Ferns. The Mamaku, or Black Tree Fern, is the country's largest, and can grow to 20m (65ft) high. Its massive fronds grow up to 6m (20ft) long and 2m (6ft) wide. Ferns are prominent in many parts of New Zealand, but particularly in the forests. Including tree ferns, New Zealand has nearly 200 species.

Despite its southerly position, New Zealand does have native palm trees. The Nikau is the world's southernmost palm, and can be found growing in the wild to around halfway down the South Island.

Away from the coasts and forests are some large areas of native grasslands, particularly in the South Island east of the Southern Alps. These grasses mainly form in clumps known as tussocks. There are dozens of species, with a wide range of colours including green, yellow, red and blue. The huge Toetoe, a type of native pampas, has flowers that reach 6m (20ft).

Nearly half of New Zealand's native plant species are alpine plants, often only found above the bush line at an altitude that makes conditions too harsh for forest flora. The many and varied alpine plants include several flowering ones (white and yellow are the dominant colours), and the unusual Pygmy Pine whose larger examples barely reach half a metre (1.6ft) in height. Evolving in isolation has made many of these alpine species unique to New Zealand.

PEOPLE

New Zealand is a country of immigrants. It was one of the last places on the globe to be settled by humans, with the Moahunters arriving in about the ninth century, and Maori arriving around the mid-14th century. By the mid-1600s the Europeans had also found New Zealand, although it was another two centuries before they settled in any great numbers. Since then the country has been influenced by people of many cultures, who have gradually assimilated into a nation of nearly four million people. While some have retained individual characteristics and culture from their or their ancestors' homeland, a distinctly New Zealand culture has also slowly developed.

New Zealanders whose ancestors were of European descent, commonly referred to as pakehas, make up around 72 percent of the population. The earlier inhabitants, the Maori, now make up around 15 percent of the population, but marriage between ethnic groups is common so most people of Maori descent are actually a mix of Maori and pakeha. A further six percent of the population is originally from the Pacific Islands, and five percent is Asian. Together, New Zealanders call themselves 'Kiwis', after their national icon, the kiwi bird.

The Europeans

The majority of pakeha can trace their roots to Britain – mainly England and Scotland – but also Wales and Ireland. Characteristics that are important to pakeha, and to New Zealanders in general, are a strong sense of justice and fair play, and a respect for hard work and honesty. In many there can be found a quest for adventure and travel, a belief in self-reliance, and a sense that anything is achievable – all traits that were common in the early settlers, whichever country they came from.

Although many pakeha may retain some of the characteristics of their forebears after four, five and six generations, most have little sentimentality for the traditions of their ancestral homeland. As a stronger New Zealand identity emerges, links with Britain have become much weaker and less obvious, except perhaps in some more recent arrivals.

The Maori

Like many pakeha, there are a number of Maori, particularly in the cities, who have little to do with the traditions of their ancestors. However there has been a large revival of Maori culture and language in recent decades, with growing numbers speaking their native language.

Traditional Maori society revolves around the *marae*. Strictly speaking the *marae* is an open area in front of a meeting house, but the term is usually used to encompass the meeting house and all the associated buildings on the grounds. The *marae* is used to hold different kinds of *hui* (meetings or gatherings), often lasting several days, and sometimes attended by thousands of people. *Hui* are held to discuss matters of the *iwi* (tribe), and also for weddings, visits by important guests, and in particular, for *tangis* (funerals). A strict protocol is applied to the series of welcomes, greetings, and thank yous, when guests arrive at a *marae*. Advice and leadership is provided by *kaumatua* (elders) who are held in high regard for their *mana* (power and prestige obtained from respect).

A Maori poi *dance in a meeting house at Whakarewarewa, Rotorua.*

A Saturday market day in Otara, South Auckland. The greater Auckland region is home to the world's largest Polynesian community.

The Pacific Islanders

Around six percent of New Zealand's population is of Polynesian descent, particularly from Samoa, the Cook Islands, Tonga, and Nuie. Many Pacific Islanders came to New Zealand in the 1960s and '70s when the government was encouraging immigration to fulfil a labour shortage. Most have settled in Auckland, giving it a larger Polynesian population than any other city in Polynesia, and adding a distinctly Pacific flavour to this cosmopolitan city.

Regional Influences

A great many other cultural influences are noticeable throughout the country, but are often largely regional or localized. In the south, particularly Dunedin, the influence of the region's original Scottish settlers is still evident in place names, and the sound of bagpipes is not uncommon at some ceremonial functions. Further north, Akaroa on Banks Peninsula has a distinctly French flavour with street names like Rue Lavaud, as well as original French colonial architecture. Some of its current residents are descendants of the original French settlers. Other Europeans also settled specific areas. The Dalmatians came to Northland to dig Kauri gum, and later make wine, while Germans and Scandinavians came to Nelson and to the southern parts of the North Island.

Several other cultures can be noticed throughout the country including a large number of Dutch immigrants who came to New Zealand after World War II. Very noticeable are the strong English accents which seem to survive even decades after immigrants arrive in New Zealand. Although the British dominated immigration to New Zealand from the time of the early settlers, the make-up of immigrants in the 1980s and '90s changed considerably, with increasing numbers from places such as South Africa and Indians from India and Fiji. However, the main influx has been immigrants from east Asia – Indonesia, Singapore, Malaysia, Thailand, Hong Kong, Korea, Taiwan and China – who have settled throughout the country, but especially in Auckland.

RELIGIONS

Just under two-thirds of New Zealanders claim to follow one of four main Christian religions – Anglican, Catholic, Methodist and Presbyterian – although many of these people only follow their religion nominally. Of the other third, around half of these have no religious beliefs, while the rest follow numerous other religions, but none with a following of much more than two percent of the population.

Followers of non-Christian religions, including Hindus, Buddhists and Muslims, tend to be immigrants who have brought their beliefs with them from their homeland. There are several Maori adaptations of Christianity including Ringatu, based in the North Island's East Cape region, and the Ratana religion, with a following of around one percent of the country's population.

EDUCATION

Education in New Zealand is of a high standard, with many thousands of overseas students coming to the country's universities and institutions to study, and in particular to learn English.

As well as seven universities, there are 25 polytechs, which together cater for around 200,000 students, and about

In the country's most English city, Christchurch, a tram passes the cathedral that dominates the city centre.

New Zealand's first university, the University of Otago (Dunedin), continues to grow in reputation and student numbers.

700,000 pupils attend primary and secondary schools – which are both free and compulsory.

LANGUAGES

New Zealand has two official languages, English and Maori. Virtually all citizens speak English, while a large number of Maori people and a few pakeha speak Maori, which is often exclusively used on *maraes*. Maori is a Polynesian language, not dissimilar to the languages of Hawaii and French Polynesia. It is not uncommon to hear Maori words in the middle of English sentences, especially when they have no exact English translation – for instance, *whanau* (extended family), or *mana* (a mix of respect, power and esteem). Maori greetings are also often used – *kia ora* (hello) and *haere mai* (welcome). In the past, Maori children were punished for speaking their native language at school, but now it is widely taught and all government departments have both English and Maori titles.

Maori place names are widely used throughout New Zealand, and always have been. However many of the major landmarks have European names, and in recent years there has been a tendency to reinstate original Maori names. An example is Mt Taranaki, formerly Mt Egmont. At first many pakeha were strongly against this, but over time, and as ties with Europe and Britain in particular become weaker, most New Zealanders have happily adjusted to names that have more of a New Zealand identity.

Most Maori names are descriptive, either of a place or event. Commonly used prefixes and suffixes include *wai* (water), *roto* (lake), *puke* (hill), *moana* (ocean or lake), *whanga* or *wanga* (harbour, inlet or bay), *awa* (river or valley), *tara* and *maunga* (mountain), *motu* (island), *hau* (wind), and *kai* (eat). These descriptions are usually qualified with one or more words including *nui* (big), *iti* (small), *roa* (long or high), and *rau* (many). In this way Rotoiti becomes 'small lake', Rotoroa is 'long lake', Wanganui is 'big harbour', and Pukerau is 'many hills'. Many places have much longer and more evocative names, but are shortened to a usable length. The ultimate example is Taumata-whakatangihangakoauauotamateapoka-whenakitanatahu – itself supposedly a shortened version of an even longer name, but commonly shortened to 'Taumata'. There is more than one translation of the name, claimed to be the world's longest, including: 'The place where Tamatea, the man with the big knees, who slid, climbed and swallowed mountains, known as Landeater, played his flute to his loved one'; and 'when Tamatea's brother was killed in a battle near here, Tamatea climbed this ridge and played a lament on his flute'.

LIFESTYLE

Most New Zealanders enjoy a lifestyle that would be the envy of people the world over. While national income does not rate all that highly when compared to some industrialized nations, there are benefits to living in a temperate country, roughly the size of the United Kingdom, but with less than 10 percent of the population. Houses are often built on sizable plots of land sometimes referred to as a 'piece of paradise', but more commonly 'the quarter-acre block' – a term that is widely used despite the change to the metric system of measurement during the 1960s and '70s. The majority of houses are bungalows; single-storey free-standing houses on their own section, often with large flower and vegetable gardens. Terrace houses, semi-detached units, and apartment blocks don't have the sense of space that Kiwis require, and are seldom seen outside major cities in New Zealand.

The Great Outdoors

New Zealanders have a love affair with the 'great outdoors', which is not surprising as some of the world's most stunning scenery is virtually at their back door. Clean air and vast wilderness areas draw people to the 'bush' – the label New Zealanders fondly give to their forests.

There is a vast network of scenic walks across the country, ranging from five-minute strolls to more strenuous hikes that take several days, like the Milford, Routeburn and Heaphy tracks. For Kiwis a long walk of more than a day, usually staying overnight in back country huts, is called 'tramping'. A large percentage of the population goes tramping at some stage in their lives – it is not a pastime restricted to the fit and hardy.

On holiday weekends camping and caravanning are very popular, and many New Zealanders own holiday houses, often near beaches, lakes or rivers. These are called baches, although in the far south they are known as cribs. In

summer, watersports like fishing, boating, water skiing, kayaking and yachting are popular.

Sport and Travel

No sport is more passionately followed than rugby, which is often labelled the national game. Players in the national team, the All Blacks, become automatic celebrities. A great variety of other sports are also played, and being very aware of their small population, New Zealanders will make heroes of any Kiwi who becomes a world champion.

Of particular note are a number of highly respected people like Sir Edmund Hillary who was the first mountaineer to climb Mt Everest, and Sir Peter Blake whose team won yachting's Americas Cup. The name of Bruce McLaren, a distinguished racing car driver and engineer, lives on in the Formula One McLaren racing team long after his death in 1970.

Like many countries who are close neighbours, New Zealanders have a love/hate relationship with Australia when it comes to sports. While fiercely competitive when playing each other, both countries will usually back their trans-Tasman cousins when one is competing against a larger northern hemisphere rival.

Above: *Skiing and snowboarding are popular winter sports.*
Below: *The 'national' game, rugby.*

Travel is another great Kiwi pastime. Approximately one-third of the population travels overseas every year – a high percentage considering how isolated New Zealand is (airfares are costly). The small population and the country's isolation provide a strong impetus for travel. Many leave home for a year or more on what is referred to as the great 'O.E.', or 'overseas experience'.

Kiwi Ingenuity

Another trait in the Kiwi character shaped to some extent by isolation, is inventiveness. 'Kiwi ingenuity' and 'number eight wire' are frequently used terms. It is claimed, not completely in jest, that anything can be made with a piece of #8 wire (standard fencing wire), and this product has effected many a desperate repair on farms and roadsides around the country. From a pioneering past when equipment was simply not obtainable, until relatively recent times when imported machinery was expensive and parts sometimes difficult to get, a 'do-it-yourself' attitude has become a strong New Zealand tradition.

An allegedly New Zealand invention that is still controversial is that of the aeroplane. It is claimed that the first aeroplane was successfully flown by a south Canterbury farmer, Richard Pearce, and that the first powered flight by his home-built plane, with a home-built engine, occurred on 31 March 1902, 21 months before the Wright brothers' successful flight. Pearce's flight lasted for around a kilometre (0.6 of a mile) before he crashed, and was witnessed by nine people. It has never been recognized, however.

Another south Canterbury farmer, William Hamilton, invented the jet boat in the 1950s. This propellerless boat, which is powered by a water pump, is used world wide — especially in shallow waters or where divers or marine life would otherwise be endangered by propellers.

Other New Zealand firsts include Lord Rutherford's splitting of the atom in the 1930s, and in the same decade the pioneering solo flights of aviatrix Jean Batten, between England, Australia and New Zealand, as well as countries in Asia and South America. There have been several significant achievements in the medical field, including the first pre-natal blood transfusion and the first heart valve transplant.

Above: *A rugged landscape has led to several Kiwi inventions, including the ski-plane and* (below) *the jet boat.*

In the agricultural sector, New Zealand inventions include the electric fence, net-guns to catch wild deer, milking machines, and a dart gun and tranquillizer dart which uses a disposable syringe (the latter is now used more widely in the medical profession).

Yet another flying first was the use of skis on planes to land in alpine regions – and of course the enormously popular sport of bungy jumping.

ARTS

It has often been said that New Zealand art has looked outside the country for stimulus and leadership, and again for approval. Although a generalization, and certainly not fair on a great many individuals, the criticism to a large extent reflected the character of the pakeha majority in New Zealand. Despite being in New Zealand for generations, strong links were maintained with Britain, and only as those ties have weakened has New Zealand found its own identity.

At the same time the Maori, with many of their traditions starting to fade away as they became 'Europeanized', put great effort into a revival of their language and culture. In the past, traditional Maori arts have not always been appreciated as the true *taonga* (treasure) that they are.

It is now widely accepted that New Zealand art has come of age, no longer looking to European roots, and finding inspiration and originality within its own borders. At the same time, many classical arts are retained. The New Zealand Symphony Orchestra and the New Zealand Ballet Company receive government and corporate sponsorship, enabling them to tour the country — something that would not otherwise be commercially feasible given New Zealand's small population. There are internationally renowned opera stars like Dame Kiri Te Kanawa and Dame Malvina Major, not to mention a number of up-and-coming stars.

Well-known New Zealand writers include Katherine Mansfield, Dame Ngaio Marsh, Janet Frame and Frank Sargeson, as well as poet James K Baxter. Writers who have enjoyed success in recent times include Witi Ihimaera, and Keri Hulme whose novel *the bone people* won the prestigious international Booker Prize. Janet Frame's autobiographical *An Angel at My Table* (1984) was made into an acclaimed film by Australian-based New Zealand director Jane Campion.

Internationally renowned opera singer Dame Kiri Te Kanawa.

Jane Campion also wrote and directed the film *The Piano*, which won the best film award at Cannes and was nominated for nine Academy Awards (11-year-old New Zealand actress Anna Paquin won the award for best supporting actress). The film also starred New Zealand's best known actor, Sam Neill, who has featured in dozens of well-known cinema and television films including *Reilly Ace of Spies* and *Jurassic Park*. Acclaimed writer Alan Duff's first novel *Once Were Warriors* became an instant hit, and the film version directed by Lee Tamahori went on to win international film awards at Venice, as did director Peter Jackson's *Heavenly Creatures*.

In music, New Zealand band Split Enz and band member Neil Finn's subsequent band, Crowded House, enjoyed considerable international recognition.

At the New Zealand Maori Institute of Arts and Crafts at Whakarewarewa village, in Rotorua, apprentices are taught traditional Maori wood and greenstone carving.

A moko, or facial tattoo, is clearly visible on this historic carving at the Otago Museum. The traditional Maori moko *is actually carved into a person's face.*

Various crafts, particularly pottery and woodwork, have been popular for decades, especially with the 'do-it-yourself' attitude of New Zealanders. Until recently few people made a living from what were commonly thought of as hobbies, but with the boom in tourism to New Zealand many people can now make a living from a variety of artistic crafts, resulting in a dramatic improvement in overall quality and diversity.

Maori Arts

While the influence of Maori art takes on distinct forms, and is worthy of a book in itself, it also has influence on a great many other art forms. Likewise Maori people do not restrict themselves to traditional art forms. Opera singer Dame Kiri Te Kanawa, writers Witi Ihimaera, Alan Duff and Keri Hulme, director Lee Tamahori, actors Temuera Morrison and Rena Owen, and artist Ralph Hotere are all Maori or part Maori and are at the top of their chosen crafts.

One aspect of Maori art and culture that almost disappeared was the *moko*. The *moko* is a facial tattoo that was traditionally applied with a chisel, so that it created a permanent pattern in deep relief. As well as full coverage of the face, sometimes the buttocks and upper legs were tattooed, but on women the *moko* usually covered the chin only. Today a few Maori are starting to be seen with *mokos* again – something that, when seen in the context of a modern shopping mall, can be quite startling and fearsome. Intricate and carefully thought-out designs symbolize events or ancestors, and although modern equipment is usually used, many *moko* artists insist that in traditional fashion no anaesthetic is used. The long and very painful experience ensures that the *moko* is given proper thought and respect.

Other traditional Maori arts, though never in danger of disappearing, have also enjoyed a revival. These include music, dance, painting, oral story-telling, weaving and carving. Although dance in the form of the aggressive challenge of

New Zealand has a strong visual art scene, with its incredible scenery inspiring many New Zealanders to pick up a brush. Well-known artists from the past are Charles Goldie, famous for his detailed paintings of Maori people with *mokos* (tattoos), Francis Hodgkins, and more recently, Colin McCahon.

In many of the arts, New Zealand does not have the population base to support more than a few professionals. This is particularly true of arts like sculpting and dance. In the main centres theatre employs a small number of actors, but many theatre productions are semi-professional or amateur.

the *haka* is well known because the All Black rugby team performs it before international games, carving is probably the most prominent Maori art. The most conspicuous carvings are the highly decorated prows on *wakas* (large war canoes) and meeting-houses. These carvings, frequently on highly regarded native timber such as Totara or Kauri, often use patterns of the *koru* – a symbol very common in Maori art. A motif with a bulbed end, the *koru* is often said to resemble an unfurling fern frond, or a curling ocean wave, and is used as a logo for Air New Zealand. In addition to patterns, carvings also regularly depict faces, usually of a specific person or ancestor. These faces are seldom without a *moko* – something that in earlier days was said to be more important than any natural facial features. Parts of shells are often incorporated into carvings, particularly to represent the eyes. Another common symbol in carving is the spiral, which may also resemble an unfurling fern, but is believed by some to link Maori art to China (it is thought that all people of the Pacific originally came from Asia).

Outstanding work is often found on carved meeting-houses (*whare whakairo*) and *maraes*. Ridge poles, beams, rafters and wall panels are intricately carved with figures and patterns, symbolizing tribal history and legend. While the ancient Maori never had written language to record their history, they could carve it.

While carving was a male domain, women became expert at weaving. Woven panels of reeds are also used to decorate meeting-houses, and flax is woven into a variety of objects such as mats and baskets.

Maori art is not restricted to large pieces. All sorts of implements were commonly carved, including weapons like spears and clubs, and even spoons. In recent years pendants using Maori designs have become popular, and are carved by both Maori and pakeha, usually from bone or greenstone. Greenstone, or *pounamu*, is a type of jade found in a few isolated regions of New Zealand. It is illegal to export it from the country in raw form, but it can be bought in a variety of art forms and sculptures, including some of the most beautiful and valuable Maori art the country has to offer.

HISTORY

According to Maori legend the history of New Zealand starts with demi-god Maui travelling far out to sea from his homeland, Hawaiki, and catching a huge fish on his magic hook. The huge fish was the North Island and Maui's canoe was the South Island, with Stewart Island as an anchor.

According to scholars, New Zealand history starts with the arrival of the Moa-hunters, possibly around the ninth century. It was previously thought that the Moa-hunters were a totally separate race of people to the Maori, but now it is believed that they also came from east Polynesia, and may have been early Maori or, at least, related to them.

The Maori

In Maori oral history the mythical figure of Kupe reached New Zealand in 925AD, and then returned to Hawaiki (thought to be one of the French Polynesian islands) with sailing directions. The Maori naming of New Zealand, Aotearoa – land of the long white cloud – is attributed to Kupe's wife. Tradition has it that after a period of severe conflict in Hawaiki, a great fleet of eight war canoes set off, landing in Aotearoa in about 1350AD. It is to this fleet that modern Maori trace their ancestors.

The life of the Maori in Aotearoa was tribal and at times also extremely violent. Warriors were trained for battle from an early age, and the losers in battle were often slain, had their heads cut off and preserved, and were also sometimes eaten. Life expectancy was low, about 20 to 30 years, but Maori society was nevertheless highly developed in the arts of tattooing, carving and weaving.

An illustration from Abel Tasman's 1642 diary depicts his first contact with Maori. After a violent skirmish, Tasman called the place Murderers' Bay, which is today called Golden Bay.

Above: *The New Zealand flag being raised at Waitangi's Treaty House.*
Below: *Maori chief Hone Heke; he cut down the British flagpole at Russell four times.*

The First Europeans

The first European to sight New Zealand was Dutch Captain Abel Tasman, who in 1642 sighted the point that is now Cape Foulwind near Westport in the South Island. Although he put New Zealand on the map he never actually set foot in the country, wary of Maori warriors after his ship's boat was attacked in Golden Bay.

The country was briefly known to Europeans as Staten Land, as it was believed to be part of South America. Then it was given the Latin name Zeelandia Nova, but was changed to the Dutch version, Nieuw Zeeland, after the Dutch province of Zeeland.

It was nearly 130 years later before the next European ship, under the command of Captain James Cook, 're-discovered' New Zealand in 1769. In his ship, the *Endeavour*, Cook spent six months accurately charting the New Zealand coastline. He did make one or two mistakes – marking Stewart Island as a peninsula and Banks Peninsula as an island. Cook's landing at Gisborne preceded Frenchman Jean-François Marie de Surville's landing in Northland by just two months.

In the 1790s sealers and whalers arrived in New Zealand, but within a few short decades the once plentiful whales and seals had virtually been wiped out. During this period, inter-action between Europeans and Maori had resulted in a marked decline in the Maori population. Europeans brought diseases to which the Maori had no immunity, and they also brought fire-arms which warring tribes used to decimate each other.

Missionaries arrived in the early 1800s and with them came domestic farm stock, and new farming methods which many Maori quickly adopted, although they were significantly slower to take up Christianity. In 1815 Thomas King became the first European child to be born in New Zealand, and by the 1830s European colonization was in full swing.

Captain James Cook

Land Wars

By 1840 there was a need for a formal agreement between the British and the Maori to stop the often violent disagreements over land. Another problem the British faced was the general lawlessness of many settlers, as well as the threat of settlement by the French, who landed at Akaroa on Banks Peninsula in 1840, on a piece of land they had bought two years previously.

On 6 February 1840, the Treaty of Waitangi was signed, guaranteeing Maori land rights in exchange for British sovereignty. This treaty is arguably still the country's most important, and controversial, document. In 1840 the capital was also moved from Russell in the Bay of Islands (the site of the first European settlement), to Auckland, which remained the capital for 25 years.

Hone Heke, the first chief to sign the treaty, was not happy about the moving of the capital and the resulting economic downturn. He also resented the ex-pansionism of the British. In a show of defiance he cut down the flag pole at Kororareka (Russell) four times during the period 1844 to 1845. The Treaty of Waitangi did not stop Maori losing their lands to settlers and the government, and this led to a build-up of tension

With a rush to the inland goldfields of Otago after 1861, the city of Dunedin prospered from its position as a major staging post. Shown here is Cobb's Coach, outside the Empire Hotel.

and occasional violence in the two decades following its signing.

Over this period there was also an influx of settlers into the new colony, which by 1858 had a population of 115,000, with more settlers than Maori. This put further pressure on land and led to the establishment of the Maori King movement. Several Maori tribes, unable to stop settlers encroaching onto their lands, banded together, with the idea that a unified front would make their position stronger, and chose an elderly Waikato chief, Te Wherowhero, as their first king.

During the 1860s there were land wars in various places in the North Island, with the most brutal battles being fought in Taranaki and Waikato.

In 1861 large deposits of gold were discovered in Otago in the South Island. Hopeful prospectors came from other parts of the country, but also from Australia and the rest of the world. The coastal city of Dunedin flourished with the inland gold rush, and the country's first university was founded there in 1869. Although the initial gold rush died down, and despite a depression in the 1880s, the region was the country's most prosperous for half a century.

Birth of a Modern Nation

In 1865 the capital was moved again, this time from Auckland to Wellington, and two years later the Maori were given their own representation in parliament. In the 1870s the country embarked on ambitious public work schemes, borrowing £10 million to do so, and by the end of the decade there were nearly 2000km (1200 miles) of railway, and free public schooling had been established. The major centres on the North and South islands were linked by telegraph and a line stretched all the way to Australia, which connected New Zealand to Britain.

By 1880 the population had reached half a million, and development continued through the decade with electricity and street lights being supplied to many towns, and the first refrigerated shipments of meat to Europe. However, the decade also saw difficult times, and the workers' unions gained power. In Dunedin, The Tailoresses Union was formed to improve the terrible working

One of New Zealand's newest landmarks is the huge Sky Tower (328 m; 1076 ft) in central Auckland, completed in 1997.

conditions of seamstresses. Previously, in 1878, New Zealand had been the first country to legalize unions, though some professions and trades had been working an eight-hour day since 1840.

The Christian Women's Temperance Union, led by Kate Sheppard, eventually won women the right to vote after several attempts at petitioning parliament. This was passed into law in 1893, making New Zealand the first country in the world to do so, 25 years ahead of both the United Kingdom and the United States of America.

Five years later New Zealand also had the world's first old age pension.

New Zealand at War

Between 1899 and 1902, New Zealand backed Britain in the Boer War in South Africa. It was the first overseas war that New Zealand troops had fought in. By 1910 the population had reached a million, but soon the country was back at war again, suffering terrible losses in World War I. New Zealanders fought

Jets on a military exercise fire live rockets above a training ground in the region of Mt Ruapehu, near the country's principal army base.

beside Australians at Gallipoli in Turkey, in a campaign (ordered by Churchill) which was doomed to failure. ANZAC (Australia and New Zealand Army Corp) troops landing at Anzac Cove on 25 April 1915 were slaughtered in large numbers. This day is now a national holiday to remember those who died. The horrific situation led to the development of a strong bond between the South Pacific neighbours, and strangely enough, also with the Turks in later years.

In World War I, around 17,000 of New Zealand's 100,000 troops were killed, and there were 58,000 casualties – a total of more than seven percent of the country's population.

More tragedy was to strike New Zealand at the end of the war. In an influenza epidemic at its worst in November 1918, it is thought that 8500 people died, though the official death toll was 6700. The Maori were particularly hard hit with one death in every 25 people.

At the end of the war there was a move towards the prohibition of alcohol throughout the country. In 1917 a law had been passed banning the sale of alcohol after 18:00. Workers rushing to have a drink after work led to the coining of the term 'six o'clock swill', and the law stayed in force for half a century until 1967. A vote to completely ban alcohol nearly succeeded in 1919, and was only defeated by a small margin because of the extra votes from overseas servicemen.

One of the country's worst natural disasters happened in 1931. The Hawke's Bay earthquake, often called the Napier earthquake, destroyed the towns of Hastings and Napier, resulting in 256 deaths. The 1930s were also the depression years – a very difficult decade for New Zealanders with widespread unemployment, resulting in rioting in some large centres.

When World War II broke out in 1939, New Zealand sent forces to fight in

North Africa and Italy. Later, in 1941, New Zealanders went to fight in the Pacific after Japan bombed Pearl Harbour. As was the case in World War I, New Zealand forces gained a reputation as courageous and skilled combatants, including around 11,000 aircrew who fought in the British Royal Air Force.

The Prosperous 1950s and '60s

During the war, many aspects of the New Zealand economy improved. The massive effort of workers increased production in many areas, but there were shortages of imports, and wages stayed low as did inflation, greatly improving New Zealand's financial position. In the post-war years the trend continued, and there was increased immigration from Europe with the population passing the two million mark in 1952.

The following year New Zealand climber Edmund Hillary and Sherpa Tenzing from Nepal became the first

Left: *Luxury yachts at Westhaven Marina in New Zealand's largest and most populous city, Auckland.*
Below: *In many rural areas population drift to the cities has led to a downturn.*

team to reach the summit of the world's highest mountain, Mt Everest.

During the 1950s and '60s, New Zealand soldiers were involved in the Korean and Vietnam wars, but overall the decades were a prosperous time. However, there were also two major transport disasters. In the Tangiwai disaster in 1953, 151 people were killed when a mud flow from the erupting Mt Ruapehu washed away a railway bridge; and in 1968, during a severe storm the passenger ferry *Wahine* hit rocks at the entrance to Wellington Harbour and 51 people drowned.

Mixed Fortunes – the '70s and '80s

The 1970s saw a declining economy and increasingly severe government measures to halt this. 'Think Big' projects like the large Clyde dam created a number of medium-term jobs, but cost overruns and massive foreign loans made the overall benefit of these projects doubtful. 'Carless' days, where cars were banned from use for one day per week, were introduced in 1979 as a measure against the international oil shortage crisis. In the same year New Zealand had its worst ever disaster in terms of loss of life. An Air New Zealand DC10 on a sightseeing trip smashed into the side of the 3794m (12,448ft) volcano, Mt Erebus, in Antarctica. None of the 257 passengers and crew on board survived.

The tour of the South African Springbok rugby team in 1981 saw some of New Zealand's worst civil disturbances of the 20th century. There were huge demonstrations and riots as South Africa's apartheid system polarized the New Zealand public. Thousands protested against the tour, but there were also thousands who thought that politics had no place in sport and the Springbok tour should go ahead. There were also heavy clashes between demonstrators and police. In the following year, the government tried to artificially control the worsening economy and high inflation by freezing wages, rents and prices of goods, making any increases unlawful.

A snap election in 1984 brought a Labour government to power, with a popular promise of banning nuclear-powered or armed ships from New Zealand waters. However, because of the policy, New Zealand was threatened with (amongst other things) expulsion from the ANZUS (Australia/New Zealand/United States) defence agreement. Despite intense pressure, New Zealand stuck to its anti-nuclear stance, gaining international recognition for this.

In 1985 the Greenpeace ship *Rainbow Warrior* was blown up in Auckland, resulting in the death of a Portuguese photographer. It was found that France had planned and carried out this terrorist attack, and also that the United

Kingdom and the United States knew of the impending bombing but did nothing to stop it. Two members of the group responsible were caught by the New Zealand authorities and were sentenced to imprisonment. However, after France threatened to destroy New Zealand trade in Europe, which would potentially bankrupt the country, the matter went to arbitration and ended in a deal that France later reneged on.

The late 1980s also saw the start of a complete overhaul of the New Zealand economy and infrastructure. Government departments were privatized, a new goods and services tax (GST) was introduced and subsidies were abolished. Drastic reforms continued in the 1990s – a decade when the government started to address Maori protests about land illegally confiscated one and a half centuries previously, with compensation packages including land, money and customary rights.

GOVERNMENT

Although originally based on the British or Westminster system of government, the New Zealand government has gradually cut its ties with Britain, and there is talk about the possibility of it becoming a republic. Today Britain has little influence on New Zealand, although constitutionally the British Monarch is head of state, and the highest court of appeal is the British Privy Council, though appeal proceedings seldom progress this far.

Currently, New Zealand has 120 elected members of parliament. From these members, the Prime Minister chooses cabinet ministers to be in charge of

various portfolios. Although the cabinet is the top council in government, new legislation is required to be passed by parliament. Above the Prime Minister is the Governor-General who is the Queen's representative and is largely, but not completely, a figurehead. It is conventional for the Governor-General to keep out of politics, and not to make any political statements. However, his or her signature is required on new legislation and in exceptional circumstances he or she has the power to dismiss the Prime Minister or to dissolve parliament.

A new electoral system, Mixed Member Proportional representation (MMP), was chosen by the New Zealand public

Top: *Legislation chamber, Parliament buildings, Wellington.* Above left: *Richard Seddon, prime minister from 1893–1906, near 'The Beehive'* (above), *newest of the parliament buildings.*

Waitangi Treaty House, Waitangi, Bay of Islands – where the country's founding document was signed by representatives of the British empire and Maori chiefs in 1840.

and introduced in 1996. The new system still uses a maximum three-year term between elections, but adults over 18 years old now have two votes; one for a local candidate in their electorate, and a second vote not for an individual but for the political party they prefer. In this way just over half of the 120 elected Members of Parliament come from local electorates; and the rest are chosen from political party lists to make up a parliament that corresponds to the public's second (party) vote.

People of Maori descent may enlist on a separate electoral list if they wish, to vote for special electorates reserved for Maori candidates. There are usually four or five Maori electorates, depending on how many voters are registered on the Maori list. The separate electorates were brought in to make sure that Maori had fair representation in parliament since despite having large numbers, they are a minority in virtually all electorates.

New Zealand does not have a single written constitution, but instead has a mix of convention, protocols, and parliamentary acts, including the Bill of Rights Act and the Human Rights Act.

The Treaty of Waitangi

The Treaty of Waitangi, signed on 6 February 1840 (now the national day, Waitangi Day), is considered by most New Zealanders to be the country's founding document. This document gave Maori rights and protection as citizens, in return for ceding sovereignty of the country to the Queen of England. Although their lands were protected, they could sell them at a mutually agreed price.

One major problem with the treaty is that there are differences between the Maori and English versions, leading to different interpretations. For instance, in the English version Maori ceded sovereignty, while in the Maori version they ceded governorship but retained chieftainship of their lands. New Zealand was also not a cohesive country at the time, but a group of tribal territories, so there was no ultimate Maori authority to cede power to the Queen. Not all the chiefs signed the treaty, and others did not even see it.

As time passed the treaty was virtually forgotten and a large amount of Maori land was taken, confiscated and stolen by the government and settlers. The treaty was only 'found' in the early 20th century, and its importance has slowly been accepted by government since then. Despite the suspicions of some – both Maori and pakeha – that the Treaty is fraudulent in its intent, few indigenous people worldwide received similar written guarantees from colonial powers. This has allowed the Maori to demand what was promised to them in the Treaty in 1840, namely that land would only change hands when a fair price was agreed upon, and finally Maori are starting to receive recompense for the lands which were taken illegally from them.

The Armed Forces

During the 20th century New Zealand has also seen violent conflict, though not internally. New Zealanders fought in World Wars I and II, the Vietnam War, and in recent times peace-keeping forces have worked in Africa, Bosnia, and Papua New Guinea. Today New Zealand's defence forces consist of an army, navy and airforce, with a total combined permanent staff of around 10,000. Although numbers are small and equipment is relatively unsophisticated, members of the forces are highly trained and defence ties with Australia are strong.

International Relations

The country's refusal to let nuclear-armed or powered ships into its ports since the mid-1980s has greatly upset the USA, but is highly popular within the country, and is gaining widespread support around the globe. Despite the cooling of defence relations with the USA, the country remains New Zealand's second biggest import partner and third biggest export partner. Australia is top in both categories. Recent decades have seen a reduction in the reliance on Britain (which is fourth) and closer relations with Asia, in particular Japan.

ECONOMY

During the 1980s and '90s the New Zealand economy underwent major restructuring which involved large-scale privatization of government organizations including railways and telecommunications, amongst others. Regulations and subsidies have been replaced with free market and 'user pays' policies. The Employment Contracts Act, introduced in 1991, took power away from unions with workers having to negotiate their individual contract, resulting in cheaper labour.

The restructuring led to a resurgence in the economy, helped by large-scale

Dairy farming and dairy products are a billion-dollar industry.

foreign investment. However, a large percentage of workers have had cuts in pay, conditions and job security. The deregulation has covered virtually all sectors, including health and education, and many services previously supplied by government now have to be paid for.

On the positive side there have been benefits for consumers buying imported goods as a result of the lower tariffs and taxes.

New Zealand imports electrical goods and machinery, particularly in the transport sector, as well as petroleum products. While some high-technology machinery is made in New Zealand, it is often of a specialized nature and produced on a smaller scale. The country does not have the population base to enable it to mass-produce some goods.

AGRICULTURE

One of the mainstays of the New Zealand economy is agriculture, especially when it comes to exports. Meat, wool, dairy products and fruit, along with timber products and fish, make up the majority of New Zealand's export earnings.

Considerable emphasis has been put on research and development in this sector, resulting in a reputation for quality in virtually all of New Zealand's agricultural exports.

Sheep, Cattle and Deer Farming

New Zealand is famous for its large number of sheep – over 50 million (and previously many more) – making it a major player in the world market for wool and lamb. While Europe, and in particular Britain, is the major market, processing in accordance with Islamic custom has opened up an important market in the Middle East. Sheep farms are found in virtually all inhabited areas of the country, from small, low country farms to massive, high country stations.

New Zealand produces over 200,000 metric tonnes of wool annually. Most of this is coarse wool, which is used for carpets, blankets, and hand knitting. However, merino sheep, which are particularly suited to the South Island's high country, produce some of the world's best fine wool. It is not unheard of for top European fashion designers to pay tens of thousands of dollars for a single bale.

The New Zealand climate is conducive to growing green luxuriant grass, making the country ideal for dairy cows. With output levels of dairy products at around a million tonnes per year, the domestic market can only consume around 10 per cent of production. The rest, including butter, cheese and milk powder, are exported, making dairy products one of the most important

commodities when it comes to foreign exchange earnings.

Exports of beef from New Zealand's herd of over four million beef cattle are also important to the economy. New Zealand beef is known for its high quality, but despite this much of it ends up in North American hamburgers.

Since deer were first released into the wild in New Zealand in 1851, deer hunting has been a popular sport. The wild population has reached problem proportions at times, however, and the government has had to pay professional hunters to cull large numbers. When helicopters began to be used for deer shooting, this became a particularly profitable business, with venison fetching high prices. As a result, numbers declined in easily accessible areas, and the attention of the industry started to focus on farming. In the 1970s and '80s, deer farming boomed and there are now over a million animals.

Stud Farming

New Zealand has been exporting thoroughbred racehorses since the late 19th century. Horses like the famous Phar Lap added to the reputation of New Zealand breeders by gaining legendary status after winning races and breaking records in Australia and America around 1930. However, in an export industry like

Horses are a common sight in New Zealand, which is known for its bloodstock.

The country's largest vineyard, Montana's Brancott Estate near Blenheim; New Zealand's wines are coming into their own internationally.

bloodstock, continuing exports are dependent on continuing wins. This is something that New Zealand trainers and breeders have managed in nearly all major races in Australia and Asia, as well as in the northern hemisphere in races like the Grand National and the Japan Cup.

Horticulture

Horticultural products are another major export sector, including what is perhaps New Zealand's best-known export, the Kiwifruit. New Zealand has led the world development of the Kiwifruit market, although the fruit is not native to New Zealand, but to China. Production and exports increased enormously during the 1970s and '80s until around 50 million trays were being exported annually at a value of nearly half a billion dollars. During the early 1990s, prices and production fell as growers in other countries cashed in on the profitable fruit. Despite this, and the reduction in area planted with Kiwifruit, the industry continues to play an important role in the New Zealand economy.

Another important horticultural export is apples, of which over 10 million cartons are exported each year to over 50 countries. Although no other fruit is exported in the same quantities as Kiwifruit or apples, some varieties, including apricots, nectarines, pears and avocados, are exported on a smaller scale, and along with cherries, peaches and plums, are sold to a strong domestic market.

Over recent years the local wine industry has grown in reputation and size. From the late 1980s to mid-'90s export sales grew tenfold as New Zealand gained a worldwide reputation for high quality wine. Also renowned for quality, and reaching similar export values are New Zealand beer and bottled mineral water.

Forestry

Another large export earner is forestry, with commercial forests covering around 1.5 million hectares (3.7 million acres). Native timber, particularly Kauri and Rimu, is valued for its high quality and was extensively logged in the early days. These timbers are still in demand, but as logging of native forests has virtually been phased out, they are often only available second-hand from demolished buildings. After earlier wide-scale destruction of native forests, most are now protected and logging has moved to forests of purpose-grown exotic species, particularly Radiata Pine which makes up 90 percent of commercial forests.

Above: *Locals and tourists enjoying the Queenstown Food, Wine and Jazz festival. This annual festival, with others in the region like Arrowtown's Autumn festival and Wanaka's biannual Warbirds Airshow, are part of the growth of event tourism.* Right: *Tourists rafting the Shotover River; adventure tourism is now an established attraction in the Queenstown region.*

Fishing and Aquaculture

Because of its relatively remote location, New Zealand enjoys the luxury of an undisputed exclusive fishing zone extending 370km (230 miles) from land. At 1.2 million square nautical miles (4.1 million square kilometres), this is an area 15 times larger than New Zealand's land mass.

Unlike much of the northern hemisphere where many of the fishing grounds are polluted, New Zealand's waters are clean. This is especially important for filter feeders like shellfish, and Bluff Oysters from the southern tip of the South Island are among the best in the world, while New Zealand mussels have a growing reputation. A rapid increase in production has occurred recently in the aquaculture industry where species such as mussels, oysters and salmon are being farmed, rather than harvested from open waters.

A large variety of commercial species of fishes are caught, and are managed by a quota system which is adjusted annually, keeping these species at a sustainable level.

TOURISM

With unspoilt scenery that would be difficult to beat anywhere in the world, as well as clean air and green countryside, it's not surprising that tourism has grown to become the number one foreign exchange earner for New Zealand. Add to this a modern infrastructure and a reputation as a safe and secure destination, and it's easy to see why tourists flock to New Zealand. New Zealanders themselves have a love of the outdoors, which in recent years has led to a boom in adventure tourism – now a major drawcard in itself.

The country has become known as the home of bungy jumping, and paying customers can have a go at just about anything from paragliding and biplane stunt flights to caving, underground rafting, white-water rafting, sea kayaking and jet boating.

MANUFACTURING

Much of New Zealand's manufacturing involves processing the major commodities the country produces. Wood and paper products are manufactured from the vast forestry resource, textiles and carpets from wool, and there are large quantities of livestock and fish to process. When the government dismantled the regulations that protected many industries, some collapsed as they found

Originally a coal-powered plant, New Plymouth's waterfront power station now uses local onshore and offshore resources of oil and natural gas to produce electricity.

POWER AND MINERAL RESOURCES

Around 75 percent of New Zealand's electricity is produced by hydroelectric plants, mainly in the South Island, using the large rivers and lakes formed by heavy rainfall in the Southern Alps. In the central North Island, production of electricity is largely by geothermal stations where generators are run by the pressure tapped from underground steam. In the Waikato region coal is used to produce electricity. Further energy demands are met by more coal deposits on the West Coast and in Southland, and by onshore and offshore oil and natural gas fields in Taranaki in the North Island. On top of this New Zealand still has to import large quantities of fuel.

Other natural resources include gold, which was taken in large quantities in the 19th century, and is still mined at a rate of around 10 tonnes a year. Silver is also mined and greenstone (*pounamu*, or jade) is taken from the west coast of the South Island. However, their quantities are such that even when combined with less valuable commodities such as ironsand, silica sand and other mined minerals, they still don't reach the value of New Zealand's gold resource.

TOWNS AND CITIES

Situated on a narrow isthmus between Waikato and Northland, **Auckland** is New Zealand's largest city. Nearly one-quarter of the country's population, around one million people, lives in the Auckland metropolitan area. In recent decades the city has seen an influx of people from the Pacific Islands, making it the largest Polynesian city in the world. It also has a large Maori population, and lately has had an inflow of immigrants from various countries in

they could not compete. Those that survived became more competitive, and recently production and exports in this sector have seen strong growth.

COMMUNICATIONS AND TRANSPORT

New Zealand has modern and efficient communication systems, with one of the most advanced telephone networks in the world. On a percentage of population basis, it also has one of the highest percentages of users of mobile phones and people connected to the Internet.

This trend on the airwaves continues with the airways, with a higher proportion of New Zealanders owning planes than occurs in almost any other country. Numerous regular flights, domestic and international, reflect New

Zealanders' love of travel, and the thriving tourism industry. Offering spectacular scenery, sightseeing flights in fixed-wing planes and helicopters are popular at dozens of locations. Planes and helicopters are also used in activities like top dressing and deer recovery, and ski planes have been designed for landing on the snow.

Deregulation of land transport in New Zealand has seen a shift from rail transport to a continuing increase in road traffic. Despite a population of a little more that 3.5 million, around 2.5 million vehicles travel the country's 90,000km (56,000 miles) of roads. Forming a link between the North and South islands is a fleet of ferries, which cross Cook Straight several times a day.

Asia, making the city the most cosmopolitan in the country.

The city's dominant natural feature is the sea, with the Manukau Harbour on the west coast almost cutting through the land to reach the Waitemata Harbour and the Hauraki Gulf to the east. This makes Auckland, often called the City of Sails, a perfect yachting venue. During large regattas it's not uncommon to see literally thousands of boats on Waitemata Harbour. Add to the scene a backdrop of the 1km-long (0.6-mile) landmark of the Auckland Harbour Bridge, or the cityscape with its 328m (1076ft) Sky Tower, and it is difficult to imagine a more picturesque city.

There are several extinct volcanic cones dotted around the city, many of which were the sites of fortified Maori villages, or *pas*. Remnants of these entrenchments are still visible today at landmark sites like One Tree Hill and Mt Eden. Auckland's northerly position and proximity to large bodies of water gives the city a warm but relatively wet climate. It seldom gets very cold or very hot, although high humidity can be uncomfortable in the summer.

On the western coast of the Bay of Plenty are **Tauranga** and **Mount Maunganui**, whose combined population is 71,000. While Tauranga is situated alongside the Tauranga Harbour, Mount Maunganui is located across the water at the end of a long peninsula that ends in 'The Mount' – the 232m (760ft) volcanic cone that gives the town its name. In 1988 a bridge joined Mount Maunganui with Tauranga, reducing the distance between them to just 5km (3 miles). Another transport link, the 1978 opening of the 9km-long (5.6-mile) Kaimai railway tunnel, combined with the Kiwifruit boom and the maturing of vast local forests, have in recent decades led to strong growth in exports, the economy, and the population of the region. During summer months the population also swells when the beaches of Mount Maunganui attract holidaymakers by the thousand.

Less than 100km (60 miles) south of Tauranga, beside Lake **Rotorua**, is the city of the same name (*roto* means lake and *rua* means two, though there are actually 12 lakes in the region). The city of 54,000 people is best known as a tourist centre because of its thermal activity. The geysers, boiling mud pools and hot springs draw thousands of people from around the world. The great Tudor-style bath house opened in 1908

Auckland city and Waitemata Harbour, seen from the Sky Tower. One in three New Zealanders lives in the greater Auckland area.

A view of Mount Maunganui from 'The Mount', looking towards the Bay of Plenty (left), with Tauranga Harbour to the right.

in the Government Gardens still stands, and is today the Rotorua Museum of Art and History. Steam escapes from underground vents at sites all around the city, including many backyards, and there is often an overwhelming smell of sulphur, giving Rotorua the nickname Sulphur City. Maori arts and culture is prominent here because of the large Maori community, and is fuelled by a strong demand from tourists.

On the east coast of the North Island, sitting astride three rivers at the point where they enter Poverty Bay, is the city of **Gisborne**. Known for its warm climate and its local wine industry, the city of 31,000 people is also an important port and has a strong local fishing industry. Being well away from the main routes between other main centres, Gisborne is relatively isolated, but it can claim a couple of firsts. It was the first place in New Zealand that Europeans set foot in, when Captain Cook landed in 1769. As

the most easterly city in the world, being the closest to the international date line, it is also the first city in the world to see the new day.

Further down the east coast in Hawke's Bay are the twin cities of **Napier** and **Hastings**, separated by just 20km (12 miles). When nearby Havelock North is included, the cities have a combined population of around 100,000 people, and support a large fruit and vegetable industry, as well as fishing and agriculture. While Hastings is inland, Napier is a pleasant coastal city, known for its Art Deco architecture. A 1931 earthquake flattened both cities, resulting in 256 deaths and the subsequent extensive rebuilding in the Art Deco style of the time. The earthquake was recorded as far away as Europe, and in a few short minutes 4000ha (9800 acres) of seabed and swamp were uplifted to become dry land.

On the west coast of the North Island the city of **New Plymouth** services

intensive dairy farming on nearby fertile green plains. Just 32km (20 miles) away is the 2518m (8261ft) volcanic peak of Mt Taranaki (Egmont). The city's main commercial interests are in the manufacture and export of dairy products, and in the exploitation of on- and offshore oil and gas fields. Oil was first discovered in the mid-1800s and a small well ran for

A statue of Captain Cook overlooks Gisborne city and Poverty Bay.

A golden dawn over Wellington, New Zealand's capital city since 1865 and ferry link to the South Island.

over a century, but in recent decades more substantial discoveries, particularly natural gas, have been made.

The city of **Wanganui** is situated at the mouth of the Whanganui River, also on the west coast of the North Island. However, the city of just over 40,000 is very much a river city, rather than a coastal city. Maori have lived along the river for centuries, revering it and using it as an important transport route. Remote upriver settlements have held onto very traditional Maori roots. The Wanganui Riverboat Centre and a working paddle steamer celebrate the Whanganui River from another perspective. The city supports local agriculture, manufacturing and fishing industries.

New Zealand's capital, **Wellington**, is situated at the southwest tip of the North Island at the end of a large natural harbour. Houses cling to steep hillsides surrounding the city which, with little suitable land to expand on, has in recent decades spilled out into the Hutt Valley and Porirua. When the cities of Upper

and Lower Hutt and Porirua are included with Wellington, it becomes the country's second largest city with around a third of a million people. The seat of government was transferred from Auckland to Wellington in 1865, and to this day there is still rivalry between the two. The main government buildings comprise the self-descriptive Beehive, a circular building of concentric floors, each one smaller than the previous (see page 36), which was opened in 1977; and the 1920s building housing the Legislation Chamber.

Wellington has a sophisticated café and restaurant scene and a strong artistic and cultural contingent. The International Festival of the Arts is held biannually, celebrating various arts including theatre and opera, as well as fringe and alternative arts. Costing hundreds of millions of dollars, the massive museum of New Zealand Te Papa (our place) opened in 1998. The museum, with 36,000m^2 (387,540ft^2) of virtual reality and interactive displays (taking a

recommended five days to see), charts the history and identity of New Zealand.

The city of **Nelson** is situated across the Cook Strait on Tasman Bay on the South Island. While Wellington often suffers from strong winds, Nelson is sheltered by surrounding hills, and is known for its warm climate and sunshine. The city supports local horticultural industries including tobacco and hops,

Cathedral Square in Christchurch city centre is a large pedestrian precinct used for markets and street performances.

as well as orchards and market gardens. Nelson and nearby towns around Tasman Bay and Golden Bay are home to a large number of craftspeople, including potters and wood-workers. The region's artistic bent is seen annually in the Wearable Art Awards, a unique type of fashion show with outrageous costumes. The event has received worldwide acclaim, drawing both entrants and audience from around the globe.

Christchurch, the South Island's largest city, is situated roughly halfway down the east coast, near Banks Peninsula. While stretching to the coast at New Brighton beach, and up into the Port Hills, the focus of the city is on the inland plain, particularly around the sedate Avon River which winds its way through pleasant city centre parks. One in three South Islanders lives in this very English city of around 310,000 residents, named after a college in Oxford. Trams circle the inner city past historic buildings and street names that have a distinctly English air about them. A tunnel through the Port Hills links Christchurch to the major port of Lyttelton, providing an outlet for the city's variety of manufacturing industries. The

city also supports the many farms of the Canterbury Plains – a large flat area that stretches north, south, and inland to the Southern Alps (50km, or 30 miles, distant but clearly visible on a fine day).

The South Island's second largest city is **Dunedin** (population 120,000), situated further south along the South Pacific coast at the end of a long harbour. The city spreads over a large natural amphitheatre – the remains of the cone of an ancient volcano – which is focused on the picturesque Otago Harbour and peninsula. Although Dunedin is a modern multicultural city, a strong Scottish flavour can still be detected 150 years after Scottish pioneers first settled here. There are a number of fine historic buildings in the city centre, built in the second half of the 1800s and early 1900s with the proceeds of the Central Otago gold rush; an era when Dunedin was New Zealand's major commercial centre. In addition to its historic architecture, Dunedin is today known for its proximity to the Otago Peninsula and its wildlife attractions of penguins, albatrosses and seals. The University of Otago has a prestigious reputation worldwide. Attracting some

16,000 students from throughout New Zealand as well as 40 other countries, the university plays a very prominent role in the city.

Although not a major population centre, **Queenstown** in the middle of the southern South Island is an international tourist destination. Situated on Queenstown Bay with nearby peninsulas jutting out into the beautiful Lake Wakatipu, Queenstown's location could hardly be more spectacular. Across an arm of the lake is the backdrop of the jagged Remarkables – an impressive mountain range soaring to well over 2000m (6500ft) and remaining snow-capped for much of the year. Behind the town, gondolas take passengers up an aerial cableway to the skyline complex for a stunning view over the town, lake and surrounding mountains. Nearby ski-fields make Queenstown New Zealand's major winter resort, but incredible natural scenery ensures the town is busy all year round. Lakes, rivers, mountains and vast rugged wilderness areas make the region an outdoor paradise – a trait well catered for by adventure tourism operators offering bungy jumping, jet boat rides, rafting, and many other adrenaline-pumping activities.

Dunedin is known for its finely built historic buildings, like the impressive 1906 railway station with its turrets and towers.

NORTH ISLAND
NORTHLAND, AUCKLAND, WAIKATO AND
COROMANDEL

Dominating the northern region of the North Island is New Zealand's largest and most cosmopolitan city, Auckland. With around a million residents – more than a quarter of the country's population – the city has distinct communities from many parts of the Pacific region, particularly the islands of Samoa, Tonga and Fiji, as well as strong influences from Asian countries of the north-east Pacific such as Korea, Taiwan, China and Hong Kong.

Auckland is a modern, fast-paced city situated on the narrow isthmus created by the Waitemata and Manukau harbours. It has a mild but relatively wet climate, and its extensive water-frontage area makes it an ideal place for fishing, boating or yachting.

North of Auckland is 'winterless' Northland, one of the first places to be settled by pioneers to New Zealand, and known for its warm climate and idyllic beaches. In the Bay of Islands, the historic town of Russell was briefly the country's capital in 1840 – the same year the country's founding document was signed at the Treaty House at Waitangi just across the bay. With over 100 islands, the bay is also a popular destination for holiday-makers who flock there from Auckland during the summer holidays.

Likewise the sheltered Doubtless Bay to the north has a similar appeal, particularly for its big-game fishing. From Doubtless Bay a narrow finger of land stretches north-west to Cape Reinga – a place of great spiritual significance to Maori, who make up a large proportion of Northland's population. Up the Tasman Sea coast of this narrow piece of land is Ninety Mile Beach – a long straight beach that is in fact nearer to 60 miles (96km) in length.

Northland is also known for its great Kauri forests. In early pioneering days Kauri gum was particularly sought after for producing a range of goods that are now produced synthetically. Today, much of what is left has been given protection, and massive 2000-year-old trees still stand in the Waipoua Forest.

Like Northland, Coromandel Peninsula to the south of Auckland also has remaining Kauri forest, and its scenic beauty and isolation make it a popular holiday spot. Its rich mineral resources have drawn mining companies to some parts of the peninsula, and have done since gold was first discovered in the mid-1800s.

South-west of the Coromandel Range and Peninsula are the contrasting fertile plains of the Waikato, synonymous with dairy farming, and the rugged steep hills and ridges of the King Country – home to some extraordinary limestone caves. The Waitomo Caves have been a popular attraction for over a century, particularly for their glow-worms and impressive stalactites and stalagmites.

It is, however, really the ocean that dominates in this northern section of New Zealand. The encompassing waters of the Tasman Sea and the Pacific Ocean regulate temperatures on the narrow strip of land, ensuring that there are no extremes.

Cape Reinga is usually considered the northern tip of New Zealand, even though that title actually goes to the nearby Surville Cliffs. A signpost (left) *marks New Zealand's isolation from the rest of the world. The Maori believe the Cape is the departure point for the spirits of the deceased. South of here, along the east coast, Pohutukawa trees fringe Coopers Beach* (top), *one of several idyllic beaches around Doubtless Bay. Further south, in Whangarei* (above) – *Northland's largest town – modern buildings in classic colonial style enhance the town basin marina.*
PREVIOUS PAGES
Page 46: *Lighthouse, Cape Reinga.*
Page 47: *Maori performers, Ngaruawahia regatta.*

The Stone Store at Kerikeri on Northland's east coast is New Zealand's oldest stone building, completed in 1835.

Some of the oldest of the great Kauri trees in Northland's Waipoua Forest on the west coast began to grow as seedlings around the time of Christ.

A memorial to the Greenpeace ship Rainbow Warrior *and her crew sits on a hill above Matauri Bay (top). In 1985, just before Greenpeace was about to protest French nuclear testing in the Pacific Ocean, French agents blew up the ship in Auckland, killing a crew member. Today the* Rainbow Warrior *rests on the sea floor near Matauri Bay as a marine reserve.*

The historic fishing village of Mangonui has always been focused on its waterfront (left). In the 19th century it was used as a whaling base and major supply centre, and Kauri gum was exported through its port.

The scenic and historic town of Russell (above) in the Bay of Islands was
very briefly the country's capital in 1840. Nowadays Russell draws people
from around the world who come to catch big-game fish, particularly marlin
(right). Off the tip of Cape Brett in the Bay of Islands is Motikokako Island
(below). Boat trips take tourists through its famous 'Hole in the Rock'.

The aptly named Bay of Islands was given its title in 1769 by Captain Cook. Motuarohia Island (above) is only one of around 150 islands that makes the region a paradise for lovers of boating and water sports. It is just 20km (12miles) from the rocky outcrops of Cape Brett (left) to Purerua Peninsula on the far side of the Bay of Islands, yet with its inlets and islands the bay encompasses hundreds of kilometres of coastline.

People flock to the Bay of Islands, particularly in the summer months when warm temperatures make diving, fishing, boating and sailing or just sunbathing (right) popular. The flagpole at Flagstaff Hill at Russell (below) is arguably the most famous in New Zealand history. Despite British efforts to protect the pole, Maori chief Hone Heke cut it down four times in the 1840s in defiance of their settlement.

To the west of Auckland over the
Waitakere Ranges, the beach
at Piha (left) has become
synonymous with surfers and
surfing. Lion Rock at Piha (below).

The tallest structure in the Southern Hemisphere is Auckland's Sky Tower. It has a revolving restaurant and four public observation decks, and at 328m (1076ft) tall, it dominates the city's skyline. For purposes of comparison, it is slightly higher than the Eiffel Tower. Far above the central business district, the view from the Sky Tower (below) over Auckland city and Waitemata Harbour is breathtaking.

Sunset (left) *from Auckland's Mt Victoria. The 70m-high (230ft) volcanic cone in the North Shore suburb of Devonport is one of several extinct volcanoes that dot the Auckland skyline.*
The addition of two lanes to each side of Auckland Harbour Bridge (below) *in 1969 doubled its capacity to eight lanes. The bridge now handles up to 160,000 vehicles in each direction every day.*

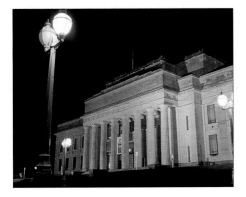

The hundreds of luxurious yachts and launches berthed at Auckland's Westhaven Marina (top) help give the city its nickname 'City of Sails'.
The Auckland Museum (above) is situated in the spacious grounds of the Auckland Domain. Spectacular fireworks displays (right) are part of several free outdoor summer concerts that are held in the Auckland Domain. The concerts, including the annual Symphony Under the Stars, and Opera in the Park, can attract two to three hundred thousand people.

Auckland is a major stopover point on the Whitbread round-the-world yacht race. These yachts from the 1998 race are berthed at the Viaduct Basin (above). Nearby the historic ferry building (left) continues to serve as the departure point for regular ferries to the North Shore and offshore islands. In recent times the waterfront (below) has been opened up to Aucklanders as a social hub of al fresco bars and cafés.

An estimated one in four Auckland house-holds owns a boat and when conditions are right, literally thousands of yachts and launches can be seen on Waitemata Harbour. Auckland's first yacht regatta was held in 1840 to celebrate the formation of the town.

Spectators view the start of the fifth leg of the Whitbread round-the-world yacht race from North Head, Devonport (left), with Rangitoto Island in the background.
Sea kayakers paddle under Orakei Jetty on Waitemata Harbour (below). Nearby on the shore, Auckland's maritime theme continues with Kelly Tarlton's Underwater World with its Antarctic displays, shipwreck displays, and a ground-breaking walk-through aquarium that has since been copied in other aquaria around the world.

A mountain biker ascends the 196m (643ft) Mt Eden (left) – another of Auckland's extinct volcanic cones. Mt Eden was once used as a Maori pa, or fortified village. Tamaki Drive (below) winds its way around the edge of Waitemata Harbour and is a popular spot for Rollerbladers, cyclists and joggers.

Modern equipment like the chainsaw have largely made the axe redundant in forestry today, however the skills of the axeman live on in the sport of wood-chopping (right) *which is regularly seen at shows and fairs. Juicy garlic prawns are cooked on a barbecue at the Devonport Food and Wine Festival* (below). *Auckland cuisine is truly international, but in particular it reflects Pacific Island traditions and the city's relationship with the sea.*

Balloons lift off above Lake Rotoroa (above) during Hamilton's annual hot-air balloon fiesta. Hamilton, located in the heart of the Waikato region, is New Zealand's fifth-largest city. The Waikato River runs through the centre of the city, where the MV Waipa Delta (left) is berthed. The paddle steamer is a reminder of the past when the river was a highway for early Europeans as well as Maori in their impressive carved waka, or canoes.

Steep hills and patches of virgin bush on farmland near Moeatoa (right) are typical of the landscape through the King Country, which extends southwards from the Waikato region.

Abseilers descend the equivalent of 30 storeys
into the appropriately named 'Lost World'
(opposite). *The strange and mysterious cavern
near Waitomo in the King Country is a spectacular abyss with its own unique underworld
environment covered in moss and ferns, far
removed from the grassy farmland above it.
When it was discovered in 1906 it was
described as an enchanting wonderland – 'a
fairyland without the fairies'. Limestone stalactites and stalagmites can take thousands of
years to be created. These majestic formations
in Aranui Cave* (above), *also near Waitomo, are
typical of many caves in the region.*
Great Spotted Kiwis (right) *are one of three
major kiwi species. The birds are very primitive,
and are thought to have been in New Zealand
for 70 million years – since the time of the
dinosaurs. They have become a national symbol
and their name is now a commonly used term
for New Zealanders.*

Large sections of the rugged Coromandel Peninsula are still covered in Kauri forest, though some sections have been cleared for exploitation of minerals, and for farming (left). *The natural beauty of the peninsula's beaches and forests has made the region a holiday destination, and also attracted a number of people looking for a quiet alternative lifestyle, resulting in the area becoming known for its handcrafts. The name Coromandel also applies to a town, harbour and mountain range on the peninsula.*

Intricate wood carvings, some taking several weeks to make, are displayed at a street market in the Coromandel town of Thames by expert carver, Adrian Peeni (above). The Brian Boru Hotel (right) in Thames dates back to 1868 – the year after the discovery of a major gold strike in the region. The town's population rose to 20,000 people, making it larger than Auckland at the time.
Sand patterns on Onemana Beach (below).

Historic graves at Ferry Landing (left) on Coromandel Peninsula document a harsh life for early settlers. Many lost their lives at a young age due to drownings, disease and accidents.
A fisherman enjoys the early morning solitude of Lonely Bay (below) near Cooks Beach on the Coromandel Peninsula.

On the east coast of the Coromandel Peninsula several settlements are dotted around the beaches and coves of the sheltered Mercury Bay. Whitianga (right) is the largest of these, and is a centre for deep-sea fishing, as well as other recreational pursuits such as yachting, kayaking, windsurfing and swimming.
Although the Coromandel is home to some top golf courses, others are more relaxed and come complete with mobile woolly obstacles (below).

NORTH ISLAND
BAY OF PLENTY, VOLCANIC PLATEAU AND THE EAST COAST

Active volcanoes, boiling mud pools and geysers are some of the spectacular volcanic features that make the central North Island such a unique region. Starting in the centre of the island at Mt Ruapehu, its tallest point, a chain of volcanoes stretches north for over 200km (125 miles), out into the Bay of Plenty to White Island.

The continuous steam from White Island, and the volcano itself, are visible 50km (30 miles) off the mainland on a fine day. Boats seeking big-game fish, as well as commercial fishing boats, trawl the Bay of Plenty waters around the island. The name given to the bay refers also to the fertile province around the coastline. This region is known particularly for its Kiwifruit, but also for its forestry and orchards of subtropical fruit.

Inland from the coast of the Bay of Plenty is the North Island's major tourist town, Rotorua. Situated in a beautiful area surrounded by a dozen lakes, Rotorua has become famous for its thermal activity and is also a major centre for Maori arts and culture. Boiling mud pools and steaming hot springs are major drawcards for tourists, as are geysers which occur in few other places anywhere in the world.

To the south of Rotorua further evidence of volcanic activity exists around Taupo. A power station runs on energy from superheated underground water, and Lake Taupo itself, which is New Zealand's largest lake, is in fact a water-filled crater – the result of a massive volcanic explosion around 2000 years ago. The lake is the source of New Zealand's longest river, the Waikato. The rivers and lakes of the whole region are renowned for their trout fishing.

Overlooking Lake Taupo are the three major volcanoes of Tongariro National Park. Mounts Ruapehu, Ngauruhoe and Tongariro are all active. In winter all three are covered in snow, creating a spectacular sight, while Mt Ruapehu, at 2797m (9177ft), has permanent glaciers near its crater lake, and ski fields operate on its slopes in winter.

Roughly parallel to the chain of volcanic activity, a series of mountain ranges largely covered in exotic and native forests also follows the major fault line between the Pacific and Indian-Australian tectonic plates and stretches all the way to the East Cape. This region's only city, Gisborne, is known for a warm dry climate that is ideal for growing grapes, used in the production of wine.

Further south, in Hawke's Bay, the area around Napier and Hastings is similarly known for its vineyards and fine wines. The two cities are also recognized for the large number of buildings built in the 1930s Art Deco architectural style as a result of the earthquake that virtually levelled both Napier and Hastings in 1931. Besides the havoc caused by these earthquakes, the powerful subterranean forces of the Pacific and Indian-Australian Plates have played a major role in creating the North Island's unique physical features – its steaming volcanic island, glaciers atop volcanoes, and turbulent mud pools – to make it one of our planet's most extraordinarily diverse regions.

Renowned for its pleasant climate and white sandy beaches, the Bay of Plenty town Mount Maunganui (above) is now virtually merged with the nearby city of Tauranga. A bridge across Tauranga Harbour links the two towns.
The blossom of the Kiwifruit (left). Near the town of Te Puke in prime Kiwifruit-growing country, a giant sliced Kiwifruit (opposite top) advertises this most important crop. In Katikati, a town near the north end of Tauranga harbour, is a series of murals (right) depicting pioneer scenes.

PREVIOUS PAGES
Page 70: *Champagne Pool, Waiotapu Geothermal Wonderland.* Page 71: *Giant Kiwifruit near Te Puke.*

The New Zealand Maori Arts and Crafts Institute, situated in the thermal village of Whakarewarewa in Rotorua, teaches traditional carving in wood and greenstone (below), and holds daily cultural performances (left) in a traditional meeting house. In a very different stylistic tradition is the Bath House (opposite) in Rotorua's Government Gardens, which started out in 1908 as a spa retreat, and now houses the Rotorua Museum of Art and History.

Lake Rotoehu (opposite) *is one of a dozen lakes in the vicinity of Rotorua. Like the much larger Lake Taupo to the south, many are renowned for their trout fishing.*
The city of Rotorua itself is situated on the edge of the beautiful lake of the same name (above). *The lake is an added attraction to Rotorua's thermal activity, which has made the town a tourist resort since the late 1800s.*

*Not far from Taupo, the secluded and exclusive Huka
Lodge* (left) *sits on the banks of the Waikato River,
just a few hundred metres upstream from Huka Falls.*

*Although the idea originally came from Indonesian
tribesmen, commercial bungy jumping* (top) *as
we know it was started up by New Zealander
A J Hackett after he made a controversial jump
off the Eiffel Tower. Today bungy jumping is
synonymous with New Zealand, and there are
many jump sites around the country, including
one at Taupo high above the Waikato River.*

*One of several thermal areas in the Taupo/Rotorua
region is Orakei Korako* (above). *As well as silica
terraces, hot springs and boiling mud pools there
is the 'Artist's Palette', pictured here.*

Situated on the shores of Lake Taupo, New Zealand's largest lake, Taupo (top) has become a popular tourist centre. Attractions include world famous trout fishing, thermal areas, and the nearby Huka Falls – which are just 8km (5 miles) from the lake along the country's longest river, the Waikato. Also nearby is the Wairakei Geothermal Power Station (above), where extremely hot underground water is turned to steam. The steam, travelling at up to 200kph (124mph) along pipes to a power station, produces five percent of the country's electricity. South of Lake Taupo is Tongariro National Park, the country's first, established in 1887 after far-sighted Maori chiefs including Te Heuheu Tukino gave land as a gift to the government and people of New Zealand to ensure its preservation. The Emerald Lakes (right) can be seen during a long but spectacular volcanic walk, known as the Tongariro Crossing, across the 1968m (6457ft) Mt Tongariro.

PREVIOUS PAGES *The Grand Chateau at Whakapapa ski village sits on the
slopes of the imposing 2797m (9177ft) Mt Ruapehu.*
Snow and small glaciers remain at the top of Mt Ruapehu (above), *even
in summer. In winter, the lower slopes become a popular ski resort,
despite the mountain being an active volcano. Close monitoring
methods using modern science can predict future volcanic activity.*

Of the three major volcanoes located in the central North Island, Mt Ngauruhoe (below) is the only one shaped in a classic volcanic cone. Along with the nearby Mt Tongariro to the north and Mt Ruapehu just to the south, all three volcanoes lie within Tongariro National Park, and all are active.

A huge 1km-long (0.6-mile) fissure was left in Mt Tarawera (left) after the top of the mountain blew off in a massive explosion on 10 June 1886. The eruption killed over 150 people and destroyed the natural phenomenon of the world-famous pink and white terraces.

Despite being 50km (30 miles) off the Bay of Plenty coastline, the 321m-high (1053ft) White Island (below) and its steam are visible from the mainland on a clear day. Helicopter and boat trips land tourists on the volcano, though gas masks are required as toxic gases continuously steam from vents.

The Bay of Plenty (right) was named by Captain Cook in 1769 after he found friendly Maori and an abundance of supplies in the region. The bay's reputation continues today, helped by its favourable climate and its prolific produce, in particular Kiwifruit and timber.

The North Island's largest area of untouched native forest (left) starts near the central volcanic plateau and runs continuously for hundreds of kilometres, virtually all the way to East Cape. It includes the massive Urewera National Park and the huge Ruakumara Forest Park.

The longest pier in New Zealand is the 660m (2165ft) pier at Tolaga Bay (above) on the East Coast. Built in the 1920s for coastal fishing boats, the pier is now mainly used for recreational fishing. The region has been hindered economically in recent decades by its location, far from any large cities and well off major transport routes, though this contributes to a relaxed, laidback atmosphere.

The city of Gisborne is located on Poverty Bay at the mouth of three rivers. It is therefore not surprising that there is a strong focus on fishing (above). This 51.4kg (113 lb) tuna (right) was landed at the Gisborne Sport Fishing Club.

The East Cape region is one of several coastal parts of New Zealand known for its surf beaches, one of these being Wainui beach near Gisborne (below). Because of its proximity to the international dateline, Gisborne also promotes itself as the first place in the world to see the light of the new day.

With rugged inland ranges on the East Cape, few towns are situated far from the coast. While the region may be considered by some to be an economic backwater it is rich in natural bounty from the ocean, including delicacies like crayfish (opposite, top right).

The Gisborne area is a major grape-growing region (opposite top left), *but has fewer wineries than other regions, as much of its produce is transported to be made into wine elsewhere.*

South of Gisborne the golden glow of dawn hits Te Mata Peak (opposite bottom). *The 399m (1309ft) peak offers great views over Hawke's Bay (the region) and Hawke Bay (the actual bay), and because of the air currents it produces, is often used for hang gliding. The house 'Coleraine' (below) on the lower slopes of Te Mata Peak is part of Te Mata Estate – one of the many vineyards in Hawke's Bay. The winery has a mix of modern and historic buildings, and produced its first wine in the last years of the 19th century.*

A view of the Art Deco city of Napier (right), *in southern Hawke's Bay, from Bluff Hill. Marine Parade runs along the waterfront and is home to a host of recreational facilities including parks and gardens, a swimming pool, kiwi house and marineland.*

Colourful business houses (opposite top) *on Marine Parade, in Napier. Mid-morning on 3 February 1931, Napier's character was dramatically and violently changed forever. An earthquake that measured a huge 7.9 on the Richter scale lasted just two and a half minutes, but its devastation of Napier and nearby Hastings was almost complete. The earthquake raised over 2000ha (4940 acres) of seabed from the ocean to become dry land, and afterwards fires raged unabated in Napier as water mains were broken. Over the following two years the towns were completely rebuilt, largely in the Art Deco style of the time* (opposite bottom right). *Despite the fact that over 250 people were killed, more positive effects of the earthquake are visible today. The city of Napier now puts a lot of effort into promoting, preserving and celebrating its Art Deco history – which has become a major attraction in itself. The 'Spirit of Napier' statue* (opposite bottom left) *on Marine Parade celebrates the spirit of the people of the 1930s.*

In late July, over 10,000 Australasian Gannets (below) *gather to breed on Cape Kidnappers in Hawke's Bay. Gannets catch fish by diving up to 4m (13ft) deep, hitting the water at up to 140kph (86mph). Cape Kidnappers was originally named by Captain Cook in 1769 when a party of Maori tried to kidnap a Tahitian crew member, possibly thinking they were rescuing an enslaved Maori.*

NORTH ISLAND
TARANAKI TO WELLINGTON

Travelling across the southern North Island from west to east, the landscape has several very distinct bands. Low fertile plains are relatively heavily farmed and populated, but in between the plains are sparsely populated rugged hills with much less intense farming.

In the west, the most prominent feature of the landscape is Mt Taranaki/Egmont. The classic volcano juts out into the Tasman Sea, with the coastline forming a semi-circle around its lower slopes to the north, west and south. Forming a full circle around the mountain, to a distance of 9km (5.6 miles) from the peak and down to a level of 360m (1181ft), is Mt Egmont National Park.

The plains to the east receive plentiful and regular precipitation, making the province of Taranaki ideal for dairy farming. The region's other major industry is the production of fuel and electricity from oil and particularly natural gas, which occurs in large deposits both underground and offshore.

In eastern Taranaki and the Wanganui region, the landscape consists of abrupt razor-back ridges and steep gullies, packed back-to-back as if the land has been crumpled like a piece of paper. In this rugged region are the Whanganui River and Whanganui National Park. The river – at 290km (180 miles) the North Island's second longest – has always been particularly important to Maori, and enters the sea at the city of Wanganui. To the east, following the main highway south from the city of Palmerston North, several larger towns and cities are encountered along the road to the capital Wellington. In this region the plain is gradually squeezed between the Tasman Sea and Tararua Ranges, until virtually all towns are on or near the coast.

The Tararua Ranges, and Ruahine Ranges to the north, are part of a backbone that runs through the North Island from Wellington up to the East Cape. Apart from roads in and around the Manawatu Gorge near Palmerston North, the ranges are not crossed by any major roads for around 100km (62 miles) or more in each direction.

The two main roads running along either side of the Tararua Ranges meet at Wellington. Situated at the end of a large, natural deep-water harbour, Wellington is known for its steep hills which have largely stopped further development of the city. Although its population is considered to be around a third of a million, less than half of these people live in Wellington itself, with the rest living in satellite cities in the Hutt Valley and Porirua.

Apart from being recognized as the seat of government since 1865 and having a reputation for its wind, Wellington is an artistic and cultural city, and has also become known for its fine restaurants and cafés. The International Festival of the Arts is held biannually, celebrating various arts including theatre and opera, as well as fringe and alternative arts. The massive museum of New Zealand, Te Papa, opened in Wellington in 1998. The 36,000m^2 (387,540ft^2) of virtual reality and interactive displays chart the history and identity of New Zealand.

The black sand of Fitzroy Beach (left), New Plymouth, is typical of beaches on much of the North Island's west coast.

The slopes of Mt Taranaki (above), a classic volcanic cone in Mt Egmont National Park, are used by hikers, climbers and skiers. The cone extends in a 9km (5.6-mile) radius from its peak. In 1986 Mt Egmont regained its Maori name Taranaki, and now both names are official. With the slopes of the 2518m (8261ft) volcano rising virtually straight out of the Tasman Sea (opposite), it attracts prevailing weather systems, receiving an incredible 7000mm (275in) of rain per year, nearly five times more than the nearby city of New Plymouth.

PREVIOUS PAGES
Page 94: *Driftwood and black sand, Awakino.* Page 95: *Experimental wind generator, Wellington.*

North of New Plymouth a series of white cliffs (below, left) *tower up to 250m (820ft)*
above the contrasting sand below. Starting at Pukearuhe, the white cliffs walking track
follows the spectacular coastline around the North Taranaki Bight.
The town of Stratford (below right), *on the eastern side of Mt Taranaki/Egmont, is a*
major access point to the mountain and a service centre for the dairy farming industry
and natural gas fields in the surrounding region. It was named after Shakespeare's
birthplace, and many street names in the town have the names of characters from
Shakespeare's works.

Over the years many small
towns on the North Island's
State Highway 1 have been
bypassed, leading to the
decline of their town centres.
However, on the bypass near
the small town of Mangaweka
in the Manawatu, an attention-
grabbing DC3 plane, turned
into a café, still manages to
stop many passing motorists.

Castlepoint, on the east coast
in Wairarapa, was named
by Captain Cook for its resem-
blance to the fortress of a
castle (right).
The Castlepoint lighthouse
(above) was erected in 1913
and is one of around 150
lighthouses and beacons – all
of which are now automatic –
around New Zealand's 7000km
(4350 miles) of coastline.

PREVIOUS PAGES *At the end of a long natural harbour is New Zealand's capital, Wellington.*
Wellington's modern skyline (above) *is partly due to the fact that the city sits on a fault line, and consequently many older buildings have been replaced to conform to strict earthquake standards. An older building that has survived is the colonnaded Legislation Chamber* (below). *It was built in 1922 and is one of three Parliament Buildings – the seat of the New Zealand government.*

The beach at Oriental Bay (right), *just minutes from central Wellington, is a popular spot on warm summer days. Its location, and grand views over the bay and harbour, ensure that Oriental Bay's houses and apartments are amongst the most expensive in the capital.*

The recent development of Queens Wharf (below right) *has turned historic warehouses into a modern waterfront amenity for Wellingtonians. Its food court, shops and cafés are popular at lunchtime, as the pleasant pedestrian precinct is a world away from busy offices and car-filled streets just across Jervois and Customhouse Quays. Office workers can enjoy lunch in the sun outside Shed 5 (below), Wellington's oldest waterfront building. The 1886 building has been given a new lease on life, and is now a restaurant, bar and fish market.*

High above the city, but linked to it by cable car, are the Wellington Botanic Gardens (below). The 26ha (64-acre) gardens include over 300 varieties of roses in the Lady Norwood Rose Garden.

While many older commercial buildings in the city have been replaced because of earthquake risk, there are still a large number of historical residential buildings (bottom), whose wooden construction is well suited to withstand the occasional shake. The great demand for land, even in the 19th century, is obvious from the very small sections. Despite even higher demand for land today, whole streets of historic houses have been preserved, adding character to areas near the city centre.

Te Papa (above and opposite right), *meaning 'our place', is the new Museum of New Zealand. Opened in 1998, it received over a million visitors in its first five months. A massive 36,000m^2 (387,540ft^2) of displays include static and interactive exhibits, temporary art exhibitions and the performing arts. The Treaty of Waitangi is considered to be New Zealand's founding document, and larger than life copies of the tattered historic paper are displayed in a special exhibit at Te Papa. 'Talking poles'* (left) *discuss the treaty from all points of view, some sympathetic, some radical, all thought-provoking. Jeff Thomson's artwork* (below), *a corrugated iron HQ Holden car, is a very popular and eye-catching display at Te Papa. For many New Zealanders, the artwork symbolizes the Kiwi character – solid and reliable but not too flashy. Corrugated iron, like fencing wire, is often used to represent Kiwi ingenuity.*

SOUTH ISLAND
NELSON AND MARLBOROUGH

Arriving in the South Island by boat, one can't help but be impressed by the complexity of the Marlborough Sounds. It takes longer for the ferry to cruise up Tory Channel and Queen Charlotte Sound to Picton than it does to cross the actual open ocean of Cook Strait. A maze of arms and inlets, almost completely devoid of access by road, makes the Sounds a favourite place for those looking for tranquillity.

South of Picton, on the Wairau Plain, is Blenheim. The town is the centre of a wine industry that is quickly developing a reputation for quality, both in New Zealand and internationally. A large variety of fruit and vegetables is also grown on the plain, and large sheep stations have been established on surrounding hills and along the Wairau Valley.

Across the heavily forested Richmond Range is the huge sweep of Tasman Bay. Sitting on opposite sides of the bay are the city of Nelson and the town of Motueka. Both are renowned for their artists and craftspeople, and for their mild temperatures and long hours of sunshine.

Further around Tasman Bay, Abel Tasman National Park has a broken coastline of golden sandy beaches and clear aquamarine waters separating numerous headlands. Recreational use of the park focuses as much on its coastline – kayaking and boating are particularly popular here – as it does on its inland forests. From Separation Point, Golden Bay forms a three-

quarter circle to the tip of Farewell Spit. This narrow sand spit stretches for 25km (15 miles) out to sea, forming a long natural breakwater for Golden Bay, and acting as a sanctuary for nearly a hundred different species of sea birds.

The forests of Kahurangi National Park, just to the south of Farewell Spit and Golden Bay, contain a similar number of bird species. Encompassing the famous Heaphy Track, the massive park covers over 400,000ha (988,400 acres) and stretches all the way from Takaka Hill near Motueka to the West Coast.

Like most of the South Island, the northern region is sparsely populated, leaving several large tracts of wilderness. Particularly dramatic are the wilderness areas of the parallel Inland and Seaward Kaikoura Ranges. The ranges are separated by a deep remote valley down which the Clarence River runs for about half of its 200km (124-mile) length. The Seaward Kaikouras rise virtually straight from the sea to 2610m (8563ft) – a spectacular sight in winter when snowy peaks tower above the ocean.

Below these ranges, the town of Kaikoura has become famous for being one of the best places in the world to observe marine mammals in close proximity. Daily trips take people out on the open ocean to view Sperm Whales at close range, while other trips take passengers to swim with seals and dolphins in their natural environment.

The Marlborough Sounds (above) are a complicated network of flooded river valleys, some of which continue inland for well over 50km (30 miles) from the open ocean. Few parts of the coastline can be reached by road, and so mail and deliveries to isolated homesteads are still arranged by boat. The rugged hill and mountain tops that survived flooding at the end of the last ice age have left the Marlborough Sounds with a very steep coastline (left). The high ridges provide a large degree of shelter for the calm waters of the sounds, making them ideal for new aquaculture industries like mussel farming.

The Spirit of New Zealand (top) *sails past the many side arms of the 45km-long (28-mile) Queen Charlotte Sound. The convoluted coastline of the sound is several hundred kilometres long, and makes up part of the Marlborough Sounds Maritime Park – a collection of over 100 separate reserves. The port of Picton (above) is the South Island's link to the north, via the Cook Strait ferries. As well as serving passengers and freight ferries, the town is the base for a number of commercial and pleasure fishing boats, and is a major access point to some of the many hundreds of kilometres of waterways in the Marlborough Sounds.*

PREVIOUS PAGES

Page 106: *The remote coastline near Whanganui Inlet at the top of the South Island's West Coast.*

Page 107: *The hull of one of the world's oldest floating ships, the 1853* Edwin Fox, *at Picton.*

Just a few hundred metres off State Highway 6 between Nelson and Blenheim, a swing bridge (left) crosses the Rai River and links walking tracks through beech forest in the 1000ha (2471-acre) Pelorus Bridge Scenic Reserve. Kayakers at the confluence of the Pelorus and Rai rivers (below) are watched by spectators high above on the swing bridge. The rivers feed down past Canvastown, named after an 1868 gold rush turned the place into a tent town, and out into the largest of the Marlborough Sounds, Pelorus Sound, at Havelock.

Marlborough is New Zealand's largest grape-growing region (above), supporting around 50 large and small wineries. Although some New Zealand vineyards date back to the 19th century, historically the country has not been a wine-producing nation. However, New Zealand wines have quickly gained a reputation for being world class. The town of Blenheim, situated a few kilometres inland from the South Island's northeast coast on the Wairau plain, has an ideal climate for growing grapes – it vies with Nelson for having the most hours of sunshine. Blenheim also supports fruit and vegetable growers, dairy farmers, and the major industry of sheep farming. Like virtually every town in New Zealand, it has a memorial (right) to those who died in World Wars I and II.

The Nelson region is renowned for its artists and craftspeople. Incorporated into a Chris Finlayson mural (above), which brightens up a Nelson boat shed, is the Maori name for New Zealand, Aotearoa. Tahunanui Beach (left), just a few minutes from Nelson city centre, is a popular recreational spot. In summer the beach area comes alive with swimmers, wind-surfers and sunseekers.
The remains of the Janie Seddon (opposite) slowly rot in Tasman Bay at Motueka. The steamship has an interesting history, having been built in Scotland in 1901 and named after the niece of New Zealand's prime minister at the time. It was used for pilot and quarantine duties in Wellington, and served as a mine-sweeper in Cook Strait during both World Wars, even firing shots in World War II.

In the north of the South Island, the stretch of Tasman Bay encompasses hundreds of smaller bays and golden sandy beaches. Some of the most pristine of these can be found in Abel Tasman National Park (above). While the park has popular walking tracks, many recreational activities centre on its coastline.

The Weka (left), despite being flightless, is a large, fast, and strong bird. Also known as the Woodhen, it is a successful scavenger and predator on the forest floor, in swamps and scrubland. The Weka is cheeky and inquisitive, as many campers have found out, after it has stolen socks, pocket knives or other small objects.

At the north-west extremity of the South Island is Farewell Spit. The 25km-long (15-mile) sand bar (above) is the result of sand and silt (some of which has been ground off the Southern Alps by glaciers) being deposited by ocean currents flowing up the West Coast. At various times of the year more than 90 species of bird visit the spit, which is protected as a wildlife sanctuary. While it is known for its stormy weather, Farewell Spit also acts as a huge breakwater, virtually enclosing the usually calm Golden Bay. Just a few kilometres south of the spit, the coastline changes dramatically into a series of rugged sandstone cliffs (right).

Kaikoura (above) *on the east coast of the South Island is a spectacular setting for an equally impressive variety and abundance of marine mammals. As well as the regularly spotted Sperm Whales* (left), *tourists sometimes see other species including Orcas, or Killer Whales, and Southern Right Whales. While whale watching is the best-known attraction, tourists are offered a variety of marine encounters including swimming with seals and dolphins.*

Kaikoura is also home to a colony of New Zealand Fur Seals, and several species of dolphin are common including Dusky Dolphins (below) in pods of up to several hundred. The name Kaikoura, taken from the abundance of crayfish in the region, literally translates to 'feed of (kai) crayfish (koura)'. Delighted visitors aboard a tourist boat (right) experience close encounters with dolphins.

SOUTH ISLAND
CANTERBURY, CENTRAL SOUTHERN ALPS AND THE WEST COAST

The central region of the South Island is dramatically diverse in climate and landscape. In the east are the Canterbury Plains – a vast flat area that is particularly hot and quite dry in summer. Towering over the plains are the snow-capped and glaciated Southern Alps, sometimes called the Main Divide – an apt name as they serve to separate two vastly different climatic zones. The West Coast, in contrast to the east, is a rugged region with an extremely wet climate and large tracts of untouched forest.

In the east of the region is Christchurch, by far the South Island's largest city. Nearly a third of the island's population, over 300,000 people, live here. The city was settled in 1850, and together with the surrounding region has a very English flavour which is reflected particularly in architecture and place names. On the plains around Christchurch are towns like Lincoln, Sheffield and Oxford, while the river Avon flows through the city itself and a beach suburb carries the name New Brighton.

Jutting out into the Pacific Ocean from the Canterbury Plains is Banks Peninsula. While the plains are alluvial, formed by numerous braided rivers flowing off the alps, this steep peninsula with its indented shoreline represents the remains of two huge volcanoes that were once an island. The peninsula's major town, Akaroa, has a distinctly French feel to it, as France's attempt to colonize the country was based in the area.

In South Canterbury, in the shadow of the Southern Alps, is the Mackenzie Country. It is an open region of tussocklands with few trees, and lakes fill several valleys that once carried glaciers. Although these glaciers have retreated since the last ice age, they still flow down from the alps, almost to the head of the lakes.

The highest point in the Southern Alps is Mt Cook, or Aoraki to the Maori, at 3754m (12,316ft). There are many ski fields in the alps, particularly in the Mackenzie Country and Arthur's Pass regions.

Arthur's Pass, along with Lewis Pass, are the only two places in the central region where roads cross the Southern Alps to the West Coast. Sandwiched between the mountains and the sea, the West Coast has a very raw feel to it. Greenstone, gold, coal and timber have drawn many tough individuals to this sparsely populated region, helping it retain somewhat of a frontier atmosphere. Suits and ties are seldom seen here – the local uniform is a heavy woollen 'bush shirt' and waterproof rubber 'gumboots'.

The West Coast, with its wild and wet weather, is renowned for the natural beauty of its rugged coastline and large tracts of rainforest still in their natural state. Birdlife along this wild coast counts the Black Petrel and rare White Heron among its species. The West Coast also has two of the world's most accessible glaciers – Fox and Franz Josef – which flow off the west side of the Southern Alps to near sea level.

In North Canterbury (opposite), *like other regions close to the mountains, there is a trend towards very large sheep stations rather than the smaller farms established on the lower more fertile plains.*

Christchurch's Italianate former Chief Post Office (left), *completed in 1879, both contrasts and complements the Gothic-styled cathedral it faces across Cathedral Square (see page 122). Between the two imposing buildings, colourful market stalls give the square a festival atmosphere.*

The Avon River meanders through central Christchurch (below) *past the town hall, making a pleasant distraction from the central business district. In a city named after Christ Church college in Oxford, England, it is perhaps not a surprise to find English-looking punters on the River Avon.*

PREVIOUS PAGES
Page 118: *New Zealand's highest mountain, Mt Cook.*
Page 119: *An exquisite greenstone carving, Hokitika.*

The Cathedral Church of Christ in Christchurch's Cathedral Square is arguably more impressive inside (left) than it is out. Although its foundations were laid in 1864, construction took 40 years as a result of a lack of funds, with final completion only in 1904. Buskers command an attentive crowd in front of the Cathedral (bottom). The Christchurch Wizard (below) has entertained lunchtime crowds in Cathedral Square for so many years that he has become an icon. The staunch monarchist delivers his opinionated monologue on a variety of topics often including political and social theory, and he is well practised in rebuffing any hecklers. He has become a tourist attraction in his own right and as such, has been made the official Wizard of Christchurch and New Zealand – a position recognized by the government.

The Avon and Heathcote rivers come together in an estuary (above) at the point where the north side of Banks Peninsula joins the Canterbury Plains. Suburban Christchurch has spread in a continuous mass across the plains and up the hills – a far cry from when Europeans first arrived in the region, when only a swamp joined Banks Peninsula to the mainland. The port of Lyttelton (right) serves Christchurch, the South Island's largest city. The port and city are connected by two tunnels through the Port Hills – a 2.5km (1.5-mile) rail tunnel was constructed in the 1870s and a slightly shorter road tunnel built 100 years later.

Akaroa (above), *meaning 'long harbour' in Maori, is one of two major harbours on Banks Peninsula. The peninsula itself is the eroded remains of two huge volcanoes, and Akaroa Harbour is what is left of one of the craters. The settlement at Akaroa is a result of an attempt at colonization, by the French, of New Zealand. They arrived just weeks too late, however – as the Maori had just signed the Treaty of Waitangi, ceding sovereignty of the country to the British – and left a small community of French people stranded in a British colony. Visitors to the harbour-side village could be forgiven for thinking they had just arrived in France, as the origins of the French settlement are still very evident today in place, street and family names.*

Despite being the site of some of New Zealand's earliest European settlement, Banks Peninsula (left and opposite) still has a wild and rugged feel about it. On steep tree-stump-studded hillsides, many farms still show signs of having been relatively recently cut out of the bush.

Unusual rock formations (above) are typical of the scenery on the road through Arthur's Pass. The pass is an historical route across the Southern Alps, connecting Canterbury with the riches of the West Coast. First used by Maori collecting greenstone, a road was built by 1866 because of the West Coast gold rush. Although not the highest pass in New Zealand at 924m (3030ft), it is the highest crossing of the Southern Alps.

At Lake Tekapo, a statue of a sheep dog (left) is a salute to all working dogs who helped make it possible to develop the harsh Mackenzie region. The statue is often mistaken for the dog of James McKenzie, the historical figure after whom the region is named – despite the spelling difference. McKenzie, with his dog, is alleged to have stolen 1000 sheep from near the coast in 1855 and driven them over mountain passes, deep into the Mackenzie Country.

The Church of the Good Shepherd (below) has a
stunning vista of the Southern Alps from its
position beside Lake Tekapo. Fed by the alps, the
lake is at an altitude of over 700m (2300ft) and
has an area of more than 80km^2 (30 sq. miles).
The Ben Ohau Range is reflected in the Tekapo
Canal (right). The canal takes much of the
discharge from Lake Tekapo in the Mackenzie
Country. Water runs for 25km (15.5 miles) before
dropping steeply through large pipes into the
Tekapo B power station and out into Lake Pukaki.

The Waitaki Valley, forming the border between Canterbury and Otago, is known for its excellent salmon fishing and three major hydro-electric schemes. The largest scheme, Lake Benmore (above), was created by a massive earth dam and at 79km^2 (30 sq. miles) is the largest man-made lake in New Zealand. In summer, the lake is popular for fishing and boating and in autumn becomes particularly picturesque when willow trees turn golden yellow. Connecting the Mackenzie Country in South Canterbury with Central Otago is the 971m (3185ft) Lindis Pass. The major road route passes steep ridges covered in golden tussock (left) – a landscape that changes in texture, shades and shapes as the sun arcs across the sky.

Often called the backbone of the South Island, the Southern Alps (opposite) are the most spectacular example of the collision of the Pacific and Indian-Australian tectonic plates – the reason for New Zealand's existence. The permanently snow-capped peaks and glaciers of the Alps run for most of the length of the South Island, providing a virtually impenetrable barrier that can only be crossed by road at three passes, Lewis, Arthur's and Haast.

The Maori name for Mt Cook (above) *is Aoraki, after a figure from Maori mythology. However, another name often used is Aorangi, which is usually translated as 'cloud piercer'.*

Trampers climb up a snow field (above right) *towards Mueller Hut in Mount Cook National Park. The hut, at 1000m (3281ft) above Mount Cook village, is a popular day or overnight climb. Mount Cook village is the access point to the peaks and glaciers in the national park, and is situated in a valley carved by glaciers* (left). *Although these rivers of ice have long since receded from the valley, there are still several nearby. Just 2km (1.2 miles) from the village, Mueller Glacier and nearby Hooker Glacier feed into the Hooker River (seen on the left). In the distance they flow into the Tasman River, which flows from the glacier of the same name.*

The Tasman Saddle climbers' hut sits perched precariously atop a peak (opposite), *high above Tasman Glacier* (below), *which is New Zealand's longest glacier. Minutes after taking off from a near-sea-level airfield not far from Franz Josef Glacier township, tourists arrive at the top of Tasman Glacier* (right), *to enjoy a snowball fight at an altitude of over 2000m (6562ft).*

At high tide, and particularly in high seas, an impressive spray of water explodes through a blowhole (above) at the Pancake Rocks at Punakaiki on the West Coast. The unusual Pancake Rocks (left) were originally formed as layers on the seabed: shallow deposits of silt with a high lime content, largely from coral, alternated with thin layers of mud. Subsequently earth movements lifted the rocks from the ocean and erosion has worn away the softer mud layers, resulting in the 'pancake' effect. The unusual coastline around Punakaiki is part of Paparoa National Park, which was established in 1987 and encompasses nearly 28,000ha (69,000 acres).

Nikau palms are abundant in parts of the West Coast, and this café in Punakaiki (opposite top) has taken its name from the native palm. The Nikau occurs to about halfway down the South Island's west coast, and as far south as Banks Peninsula on the east coast, making it the world's southern-most palm tree. The palms grow up to 10m (32ft) tall, and the upward pointing fronds have a distinctive bulbous base.

Much of New Zealand's greenstone comes from the West Coast. This highly prized and very hard stone is a type of jade and is called pounamu by Maori. A skilled carver at Hokitika (right) *turns a piece of greenstone into an artwork featuring a traditional Maori* moko. *The finest work of top artisans commands prices in the thousands, and tens of thousands, of dollars.*

The Southern Alps rise not far from the ocean, forming a barrier to moist air coming off the Tasman Sea and resulting in high precipitation and a large number of rivers on the West Coast. While some rainforest-fed rivers are stained deep brown by tannins from decaying vegetation, others such as the Whataroa River (opposite) take on a blue-grey hue because they hold minute particles of mica, which has been ground off bedrock by glaciers.

Whitebait (right), the young of Galaxias, *a native fish, are caught in nets in great quantities near the mouths of West Coast rivers.*

Sunset on Okarito Lagoon (below). Despite a gold rush in the 1860s, Okarito today has only a small isolated community, and is better known for its feathered residents, notably the country's only colony of White Heron.

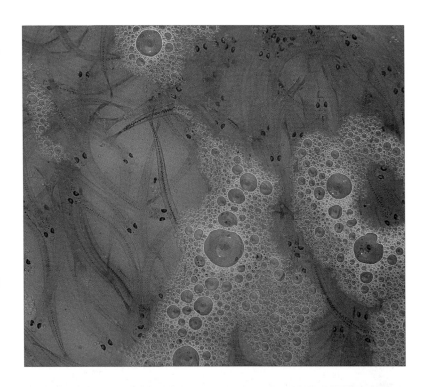

New Zealand's tallest peak, Mt Cook, towers above the clearly visible Franz Josef Glacier (above). A major tectonic fault line lies at the base of the alps, so that while the Southern Alps and the majority of the South Island are part of the Pacific Plate, the land between the mountains and the west coast – not much more than 10km (6 miles) away, and including Lake Mapourika and the surrounding plain – is part of the Indian-Australian tectonic plate.

Access to Franz Josef Glacier (left), as well as Fox Glacier just 25km (15 miles) away, is among the easiest of any glaciers anywhere in the world. From the two nearby towns named after the glaciers, it is just a short drive to the roads' ends, and the glaciers are then within walking distance.

Franz Josef Glacier (above right) *flows as a river of ice for 13km (8 miles) before turning into the Waiho River. The glacier drops to near sea level – and in the distant past it actually flowed to the sea. The unique climatic and geographical conditions that have created the glacier so close to the ocean at this latitude are quite extraordinary – the equivalent latitude in the northern hemisphere is the Mediterranean coast of France.*

At car parks around Franz Josef and Fox glaciers, the inquisitive and cheeky Kea will rip apart anything it can, and is particularly fond of car door rubbers.

A large ice arch on Fox Glacier (left) *in Westland National Park is a natural, but temporary artwork.
Continual movement of the glacier means that ice formations and crevasses are constantly formed
and broken, and can change on a daily basis. Westland National Park was established in 1960 and
encompasses an incredible variety of landscapes. The 117,600ha (290,590-acre) park includes alpine
peaks and glaciers, rivers and lakes, coastal beaches and large tracts of rainforest.*

As snow is compacted into ice, and air is forced out, the solid ice is left with a distinctly blue hue (above).
Near Fox Glacier a track climbs up though thick lush rainforest (below left) *to viewpoints of the glacier
and the peaks above it. Near the terminal face of Fox Glacier* (below right) *huge blocks of ice, some
bigger than cars, fall on a regular basis, making the face extremely dangerous.*

In 1875 pioneers arrived to take up their plots at a planned town on Jackson Bay. However, with a hostile climate and steep topography, the remote township was doomed to failure. In 1937 a wharf (below) was built to supply materials for the Haast Pass road that eventually linked the West Coast with Otago in 1965. Today only a few fishing boats operate from the wharf. The promontory of Jackson Head provides shelter for fishing boats in Jackson Bay (opposite) – one of the very few places on the West Coast that is protected from prevailing westerly winds. The remote bay is also the road end for the West Coast, with the impenetrable mountains, glacial valleys and sounds of Fiordland blocking further road development to the south.

SOUTH ISLAND
OTAGO AND SOUTHLAND,
INCLUDING
FIORDLAND AND STEWART ISLAND

Otago and Southland, which are New Zealand's southern-most provinces, are known for stunning scenery. Snowy mountains towering above crystal-clear lakes typify the Southern Lakes District of Otago, while massive glacier-carved fiords form a spectacular coastline in Fiordland, part of Southland.

Otago is accessed from the north by just three major roads: Haast Pass from the West Coast, Lindis Pass from the Mackenzie Country, and the main State Highway 1 down the east coast. The latter crosses coastal plains to run through the town of Oamaru, much of which (including a fully complete historic precinct) has been built from a distinctive, locally quarried, white sandstone.

Further south is the South Island's second major city, Dunedin. Like Wellington, it is built around the walls of an ancient volcanic crater at the end of a long natural harbour. The city's solid foundations, built on the proceeds of early gold rushes, can be seen in a number of impressive historic stone buildings.

Almost cut off from the mainland at Dunedin is the Otago Peninsula. The peninsula is gaining a name as New Zealand's wildlife capital. At the tip of the penin-sula is a colony of Royal Albatrosses. This qualifies as the only colony in the world to have been established near civilization or on a mainland. Nearby are colonies of rare Yellow-eyed Penguins, while New Zealand Fur Seals are a common sight.

Inland, Otago has areas that are scenically breathtaking, drawing tourists from around the world to the resort towns of Wanaka and Queenstown. Both are built on a lake shore facing mountains that are snow-covered in winter.

While the Southern Lakes owe their origins to glaciers, rivers of ice have left an even deeper impression in Fiordland. At the coast, giant U-shaped glacial valleys create a deeply indented coastline of fiords, with just one – the spectacular Milford Sound – accessible by road. Most of Fiordland is encompassed in the massive Fiordland National Park, which comprises approximately half of the South-West New Zealand World Heritage Area (Te Wahipounamu). The 2.6 million-hectare (6.4 million-acre) wilderness incorporates three more national parks – Westland, Mount Cook and Mount Aspiring.

In contrast to Fiordland, much of Southland consists of flat, intensely farmed land far more suited to human habitation. However the Catlins, a coastal area shared between Southland and Otago, have largely escaped settlement. Native forests have rejuvenated from milling in pioneering days, slowly drawing people to this scenic and untouched backwater.

Even more isolated is New Zealand's Stewart Island, which is virtually devoid of roads. Here, it is possible to get a glimpse of New Zealand before the arrival of humans. Around 400 residents live at the only settle-ment, Halfmoon Bay.

East of the Southern Alps, Lake Wanaka (opposite, top) is a series of flooded glaciated valleys. At the south end of the 193km² (74-sq.-mile) lake is the small resort town of Wanaka. With nearby Lake Hawea, the Clutha River, as well as other neighbouring rivers and numerous mountains, Wanaka is known for its outdoor recreational activities. Besides sports like snow skiing, kayaking, water skiing and mountain biking, rock climbing is also popular. A few kilometres out of Wanaka at Hospital Flat (left), massive boulders and rock faces look like a giant's building blocks, and the many climbing routes draw people from around the country and overseas.

PREVIOUS PAGES
Page 144: Sutherland Falls is among the world's highest waterfalls.
Page 145: Tulip farm, Invercargill.

The southern hemisphere's largest airshow (below and opposite right) is held every second Easter at Wanaka. On even-numbered years the rare and exotic planes in 'Warbirds over Wanaka' attract visitors from around the world to this small Otago town. Its population of a little over 2000 swells as more than 70,000 people pass through the gates of the airshow. As its name suggests, the airshow concentrates on early fighters like the famous planes used in World War II – British Spitfires and Hurricanes, Japanese Zeros, American Mustangs, and German Messerschmitts as well as less well-known and very rare planes.

Seen through Rolf Mills' partially completed carving 'Alpha and Omega', stone carver Ra Vincent (above left) *turns a slab of Oamaru stone into a work of art during the Oamaru Stone Carvers' Symposium.*

On the North Otago coastline between Oamaru and Dunedin are the Moeraki Boulders (above and opposite). *Some of the unusual boulders are more than 2m (6.5ft) in diameter, and unlike most rounded rocks which have been worn to their spherical state by some form of erosion, those at Moeraki have built up from a small centre. The 60 million-year-old concretions grew from an organic centre like a shell or bone on the sea floor. They are gradually being eroded from a soft mudstone bank at the back of the beach. Along the beach from the Moeraki Boulders is Moeraki township* (below). *Sheltered by Moeraki Point, the sleepy settlement, a few kilometres off the main south road, is home to a few fishing boats and holiday homes.*

Spotted Shags (above left), *nest on cliffs around Taiaroa Head at the tip of Otago Peninsula. Above the cliffs is the world's only mainland colony of albatrosses, and the only one near civilization. Also on the clifftop not far from the Royal Albatrosses there is a colony of Little Blue Penguins, though they are seldom seen as they spend all day at sea. Down below, colonies of New Zealand Fur Seals* (left) *lounge on rocks and playfully splash about in the ocean.*

The city of Dunedin sits in a natural amphitheatre at the end of the long Otago Harbour. Otago Peninsula, to the right of the harbour, lays claim to being New Zealand's wildlife capital. Among its many bird and marine species are colonies of two very special birds – the rare and endangered Yellow-eyed Penguin, and one of the world's largest birds, the Royal Albatross.

The Water of Leith flows gently past the clock tower of the University of Otago (above). The building dates back to 1878, nine years after the founding in Dunedin of New Zealand's first university. Along with the clock tower, several other historic buildings give the pedestrian precinct area of the university an atmosphere of charm and grace reminiscent of a bygone era. New Zealand is very much a sporting nation, and in addition to traditional sports, a number of more obscure sports find willing participants. A dragon boat competition (left) in Dunedin's harbour basin draws plenty of support from work and social teams, many of whom participate solely for fun.

Students at the University of Otago enjoy a warm autumn lunchtime on an historic bridge over the Water of Leith (above). The university's reputation is such that the majority of its students come from regions outside of Otago, and several thousand come from overseas, giving the campus an international flavour.

Climbing is a fast-growing sport. Away from the mountains or suitable rock faces, climbers can still find city climbing walls (right) like this one in central Dunedin.

The inspired design of Dunedin's First Church (above) is the work of prolific architect, R.A. Lawson.

After being built in 1880, the municipal chambers (right) in Dunedin's Octagon had the top three layers taken off the clock tower because of earthquake risk. However in 1989 the layers above the clock were rebuilt to conform to earthquake standards, but in the original design.

In spring Dunedin's botanic gardens are a burst of colour with mass plantings of tulips (left).

No sport in New Zealand has such a strong following as rugby. Although only around 135,000 people play the winter sport, much of the country follows the game passionately as spectators – so much so that rugby is considered an important part of New Zealand culture. One of New Zealand's premier rugby venues is Carisbrook (right) in Dunedin, locally nicknamed 'the house of pain', referring to the defeats that visiting teams often suffer. The local Otago team enjoys some of the best support for any team in the country, particularly from local university students. Important games will draw a crowd of well over 30,000 spectators, despite Dunedin's population of just over 100,000 people. Supporters of the Wellington Hurricanes rugby team (above) loudly display their allegiance to their visiting team despite being surrounded by thousands of local Otago Highlanders fans. Good-natured rivalry is all part of the atmosphere at Carisbrook, where the terraces are traditionally the preserve of university students.

The Blue Lake at St Bathans is a result of sluicing in the days of the gold rush. The lake is known for its unusual clay formations caused by the severe erosion from sluicing. Today the small lake is used for recreation, and once a year around a hundred kayakers race in the Ghost to Ghost triathlon (above), so called because of a ghost in the nearby century-old Vulcan Hotel.

The Clutha River is New Zealand's largest river by volume and at 338km (210 miles), its second longest. At Alexandra it flows past old bridge piers (left) that were built in 1882 for a suspension bridge to improve wagon transport around the gold fields.

Major industries in Central Otago, apart from tourism, are large sheep stations on the high country, and fruit orchards on lower ground. On alluvial plains around the towns of Cromwell and Alexandra, large quantities of apples and apricots are grown, but there is also a variety of other fruits including peaches, cherries and nectarines. Not far from Alexandra, Roxburgh is another important fruit region, where farmer Don Hamilton (right) *grows pears.*

Dotted in and around the Central Otago settlement of Fruitlands are numerous historic buildings, most of which date back to the gold rush days of the 1800s. Many of the buildings are slowly decaying, though a few are still used, like the Fruitlands Gallery and café (below) *which provide welcome relief for motorists on State Highway 8 near Alexandra.*

At Clyde a large dam on the Clutha River
has formed Lake Dunstan (above). Two
arms of the lake – one fed by the Kawarau
River from Lake Wakatipu, and the other
by the Clutha River from Lake Wanaka –
meet at the town of Cromwell. Dunstan
is an historical name for part of the region
and some of its features. It comes from
the gold rush days, probably taken from
the patron saint of goldsmiths, St Dunstan.

The fierce nature of the Shotover River
makes it popular for white-water rafting
(left), although in high water the river
becomes so violent and dangerous that it
is considered unraftable.

A kayaker pirouettes (right) *during a kayak rodeo competition on the Kawarau River. The river is also used for rafting and river surfing, though parts of it are so rough that they are considered dangerous for any type of water sport.*

Lake Hayes (below), *like the nearby town of Arrowtown, is known for its autumn colours. Hues of orange, red and brown colour the landscape and two species of tree in particular – the introduced willow and poplar trees – are renowned for their brilliant golden yellow, thought to be enhanced by especially severe frosts. As vineyards continue to flourish in the region, further plantings add to the show of autumn colour.*

At the Skyline complex high on Bob's Peak above
Queenstown, visitors have the choice of several adventure
activities. After travelling up to the Skyline by gondola, it is
possible to return to Queenstown by paraglider (left), or to
take a bungy jump (above) from the 'ledge'. For those not
tempted by the excitement of an adrenaline rush, a bar,
restaurant and café make the most of the stunning vista.

In the shadow of the slopes of Cecil Peak, the historic
steamship T.S.S. Earnslaw cruises the waters of Lake
Wakatipu (below). The lake rises and falls every few
minutes. Maori legend attributes this to the beating heart
of Matau – a giant monster whose body caused the
Z-shaped lake.

Queenstown and Lake Wakatipu, bathed in late afternoon light (above). *Besides the stunning views and many outdoor activities which are a feature of the area, visitors can also shop or just relax and watch the world go by at the steamer wharf in Queenstown* (below).

Mitre Peak (above), *on the left , rises steeply out of Milford Sound. With rain on up to 300 days a year, the 1695m (5561ft) peak is often shrouded in clouds and mist. Fiordland is arguably even more spectacular and mystical in bad weather, when thousands of instant waterfalls appear down the near vertical faces of glacial valleys. Situated just a few minutes walk from the road-end at Milford Sound,* Bowen Falls *(right) is one of countless waterfalls in Fiordland National Park. Few of these others are accessible, however, as a result of the rough terrain and the fact that there is only one road into Milford Sound. Fiordland has an unmistakable primeval feel to it, and its landscape has proportions that can make humans seem insignificant. Even boats on the 15km-long (9-mile) Milford Sound are dwarfed by sheer cliffs that rise straight from the sea* (opposite).

The rugged and vast landscape of Fiordland National Park can be difficult to comprehend from the ground. An aerial view (left) shows a small part of the 1.25-million hectare (3 million-acre) national park (New Zealand's largest) and the multi-armed Lake Te Anau (the South Island's largest). Few humans venture west of the lake into the wilderness area dominated by steep valleys, mountain peaks, a multitude of lakes and huge fiords.

The Milford Road travels (opposite bottom) through a landscape moulded by giant fingers of ice. From Te Anau the road comes up the Eglinton Valley on the right, past Lake Gunn in the distance, and can be seen beside Lake Fergus in the foreground. While the lakes drain down the Eglinton River into Lake Te Anau, Lake McKellar on the left flows down the Greenstone River and Valley into Lake Wakatipu. The snow line, or bush line at an altitude too high for trees, is clearly visible between the valleys on the Livingstone Mountains.

A fresh sprinkling of snow adds to the other-worldly atmosphere of the deep, glacier-carved valleys of Fiordland (above). The Milford Road is classified as a World Heritage Highway, and is particularly spectacular here in the upper Hollyford Valley before it enters the Homer Tunnel. In winter the road is prone to snow avalanches, but local authorities have become adept at using helicopters and explosives to bring down avalanches during planned road closures.

Although the road-end of State Highway 1 at Bluff is often considered the southernmost point of mainland New Zealand, that title actually goes to the Catlins. The region is a backwater of native forests, streams and deserted beaches (opposite). The sweep of Tautuku Bay (above), ending in the headland of Tautuku Peninsula, is typical of the nature of the Catlins coastline. Several rocky headlands contain fossils, and at Curio Bay a petrified forest can be seen in the rocky foreshore at low tide. The coastline is known for its wildlife, particularly penguins, seals and dolphins, while inland the 60,000ha (148,000-acre) Catlins Forest Park has renowned forest walks. Purakanui Falls (below) is one of more than 80 waterfalls in the Catlins region.

New Zealand's State Highway 1 ends at Bluff, but it is possible to continue on to Stewart Island from Bluff Harbour (above). Stewart Island (below) is approximately 30km (18 miles) from mainland New Zealand, across the often rough waters of Foveaux Strait, an hour's journey by ferry. The seabed of the Strait is famous for its Bluff Oysters – often labelled the best in the world. Local fishermen also ply the rich waters for other marine species including crayfish, blue cod, grouper, scallops and paua – a large shellfish similar to abalone. A Mollymawk (above, right) soars over Foveaux Strait near the Ruggedy Mountains on Stewart Island. Along with other types of albatross, the Mollymawk

breeds on remote subantarctic islands (with the exception of the Royal Albatross colony on Otago Peninsula). Stewart Island has escaped the ravages of the mustelids that have devastated much of the mainland's birdlife. Because of its southerly position the island enjoys long twilights in the summer, leading to its Maori name Rakiura, meaning 'heavenly glow'. This is evoked by a sunset view of Halfmoon Bay from Observation Rock (opposite). The Island's major industries, fishing and tourism, are based here. A relatively new venture for the island has been aquaculture, or fish farming, which is based nearby in Patterson Inlet.

For more than 100 years the South Sea Hotel at Halfmoon Bay (left) has been a focal point for Stewart Island's residents and visitors alike. Most of the island's 400 or so residents live near here at the only settlement. From this point it is not possible to drive much further than 4km (2.4 miles) by road. Stewart Island has around 250km (155 miles) of walking tracks. The North-West Circuit Track, which takes around nine days to complete, follows the coastline around the northern half of the island, before cutting back across swamps and tunnels of Manuka (opposite) to Patterson Inlet. Trampers walk across dunes near the coast at Mason Bay (below) on the remote west side of the island. This region, several days walk from civilization, is one of the few places where wild kiwis can sometimes be seen in daylight. Although kiwis are normally associated with the undergrowth of thick dark forests, their footprints can often be found on the dunes and beach.

INDEX